T0316325

Explaining Policy Change in the European Union's Eastern Neighbourhood

This edited volume discusses and challenges the conventional wisdoms dominating the scholarship on policy change in the EU's Eastern neighbourhood countries. Drawing upon new empirical evidence underpinning the contributions to this volume, the authors argue that compliance with, or convergence to, EU policies continue despite high costs, limited capacities and the lack of EU membership prospects. The contributions also challenge country-level or policy-type explanations that emphasise membership aspirations, asymmetric interdependencies between the EU and the neighbourhood countries, or the level of politicisation or institutionalisation characterising particular policy fields. Finally, the volume's findings point towards important differences between membership, accession and neighbourhood Europeanisation by highlighting factors that have been ignored by students of EU enlargement. These factors include the role of Russia, which is an important regional power, and of transnational actors such as multinational companies or international finance institutions, as well as the impact of informal domestic veto players on policy change in the EU's Eastern neighbourhood.

This book was originally published as a special issue of *Europe-Asia Studies*.

Julia Langbein is Senior Lecturer at the Center for European Integration at Freie Universität Berlin, Germany, and Scientific Coordinator of the FP7 research project 'Maximizing the integration capacity of the European Union. Prospects for and challenges of enlargement and beyond'.

Tanja A. Börzel is Professor of Political Science and Director of the Berlin Center for European Integration at Freie Universität Berlin, Germany.

Routledge Europe-Asia Studies Series
A series edited by Terry Cox
University of Glasgow

The **Routledge Europe-Asia Studies Series** focuses on the history and current political, social and economic affairs of the countries of the former 'communist bloc' of the Soviet Union, Eastern Europe and Asia. As well as providing contemporary analyses it explores the economic, political and social transformation of these countries and the changing character of their relationships with the rest of Europe and Asia.

Explaining Policy Change in the European Union's Eastern Neighbourhood

Edited by
Julia Langbein and Tanja A. Börzel

Routledge
Taylor & Francis Group

LONDON AND NEW YORK

University
of Glasgow

First published 2014
by Routledge
2 Park Square, Milton Park, Abingdon, Oxon, OX14 4RN, UK

and by Routledge
711 Third Avenue, New York, NY 10017, USA

Routledge is an imprint of the Taylor & Francis Group, an informa business
© 2014 University of Glasgow

British Library Cataloguing in Publication Data
A catalogue record for this book is available from the British Library

ISBN 13: 978-0-415-73883-5

Typeset in Times New Roman
by Taylor & Francis Books

Publisher's Note
The publisher accepts responsibility for any inconsistencies that may have arisen during the conversion of this book from journal articles to book chapters, namely the possible inclusion of journal terminology.

Disclaimer
Every effort has been made to contact copyright holders for their permission to reprint material in this book. The publishers would be grateful to hear from any copyright holder who is not here acknowledged and will undertake to rectify any errors or omissions in future editions of this book.

Contents

Citation Information

The chapters in this book were originally published in *Europe-Asia Studies*, volume 65, issue 4 (June 2013). When citing this material, please use the original page numbering for each article, as follows:

Chapter 1
Introduction: Explaining Policy Change in the European Union's Eastern Neighbourhood
Julia Langbein & Tanja A. Börzel
Europe-Asia Studies, volume 65, issue 4 (June 2013)
pp. 571–580

Chapter 2
Migration, Energy and Good Governance in the EU's Eastern Neighbourhood
Esther Ademmer & Tanja A. Börzel
Europe-Asia Studies, volume 65, issue 4 (June 2013)
pp. 581–608

Chapter 3
Selective Adoption of EU Environmental Norms in Ukraine. Convergence á la Carte
Aron Buzogány
Europe-Asia Studies, volume 65, issue 4 (June 2013)
pp. 609–630

Chapter 4
Unpacking the Russian and EU Impact on Policy Change in the Eastern Neighbourhood: The Case of Ukraine's Telecommunications and Food Safety
Julia Langbein
Europe-Asia Studies, volume 65, issue 4 (June 2013)
pp. 631–657

Chapter 5

Shaping Convergence with the EU in Foreign Policy and State Aid in Post-Orange Ukraine: Weak External Incentives, Powerful Veto Players
Antoaneta Dimitrova & Rilka Dragneva
Europe-Asia Studies, volume 65, issue 4 (June 2013)
pp. 658–681

Please direct any queries you may have about the citations to
clsuk.permissions@cengage.com

Notes on Contributors

Esther Ademmer, Kiel Institute for the World Economy, Kiel, Germany

Tanja A. Börzel, Otto-Suhr-Institute of Political Science, Freie Universität, Berlin, Germany

Aron Buzogány, Geschwister Scholl Institute of Political Science, Ludwig Maximilians, Universität, Munich, Germany

Antoaneta Dimitrova, Institute of Public Administration, Leiden University, Den Haag, The Netherlands

Rilka Dragneva, Birmingham Law School, University of Birmingham, Birmingham, United Kingdom

Julia Langbein, Otto-Suhr-Institute of Political Science, Freie Universität, Berlin, Germany

Introduction: Explaining Policy Change in the European Union's Eastern Neighbourhood

JULIA LANGBEIN & TANJA A. BÖRZEL

Abstract

This Introduction discusses the conventional wisdoms dominating the scholarship on policy change in the EU's Eastern neighbourhood countries and summarises the major findings of this collection. Drawing upon the empirical evidence underpinning the contributions to our collection, we argue that compliance with or convergence to EU policies happens despite high costs, limited capacities and the lack of EU membership prospects. We also challenge country-level or policy-type explanations that emphasise membership aspirations, asymmetric interdependencies between the EU and the neighbourhood countries, or the level of politicisation or institutionalisation characterising particular policy fields. Finally, our findings point towards important differences between membership, accession and neighbourhood Europeanisation by stressing factors mediating the EU's impact on policy change in the Eastern neighbourhood countries that played a rather marginal role in domestic policy change in EU member states and accession countries.

DO THE EASTERN NEIGHBOURHOOD COUNTRIES TAKE ON European Union (EU) rules for the regulation of their local markets and polities despite weak state capacities, limited democratic development and the absence of an EU membership perspective? If so, do we observe variation in domestic change across policy fields and countries and how can we explain diverse outcomes?

The contributions to this collection provide answers to these questions by examining policy change in the Eastern neighbourhood countries. We define policy change as a change in practices and institutional arrangements governing a particular policy. Since the conclusion of Partnership and Cooperation Agreements (PCAs) through the 1990s, and even more so since the launch of the European Neighbourhood Policy (ENP) in 2004, EU policy practices and institutional arrangements have served as a benchmark for policy change in the region. While the various PCAs stress the need for 'approximation of [the respective national]

This Special Section results in part from research conducted at the Kolleg-Forschergruppe (KFG) 'The Transformative Power of Europe', hosted at the Freie Universität Berlin. The KFG is funded by the German Research Foundation (*Deutsche Forschungsgesellschaft*) and brings together research on the diffusion of ideas in the EU's internal and external relations. For further information please consult www. transformeurope.eu

legislation to that of the [European] Community',[1] official documents on the ENP reveal that the EU pursues a particular concept of convergence by which all European neighbours (Eastern and Southern neighbours) are expected to converge unilaterally towards the EU model, rather than the EU and the neighbouring countries mutually adjusting to each other (European Commission 2004, 2008). Therefore, our contributions look at policy change at the level of rhetorical commitment to, formal adoption of, and behavioural compliance with specific EU policies that do not fit domestic policies. Rhetorical commitment refers to the pledges made by governments of the Eastern neighbourhood countries in public speeches to align with the practices and institutional arrangements governing particular EU policies. Formal adoption refers to what students of compliance have called the output dimension which comprises those legal and administrative measures needed to put a policy into practice (Börzel & Risse 2002). Finally, behavioural compliance is defined as the outcome dimension of compliance since it assesses the effects of the aforementioned measures on the actors' behaviour targeted by the rules (Börzel & Risse 2002). Compliance thus implicates an analysis of whether, or to what extent, Eastern neighbourhood countries act in accordance with EU policies—by way of implementing legal decisions or through changing their practices when governing a particular policy field. In this sense policy change can result in inertia, incomplete or complete compliance with EU policies as the formal adoption and implementation of promoted policies might allow for adjusting policies to national peculiarities (Ademmer & Börzel, in this collection). At the same time, we find policy change giving rise to incomplete or complete convergence with EU policies (Dimitrova & Dragneva; Buzogány; Langbein, all in this collection). How do we account for such variation?

The literature tends to be rather sceptical regarding the likelihood of policy change that results in compliance and convergence with EU policies. First, compared to the EU candidate countries from Central and Eastern Europe, the EU's Eastern neighbours have weaker regulatory capacities and score lower in terms of democratic development (Börzel & van Hüllen 2011). At the same time, the Eastern neighbours face a situation characterised by a high degree of incompatibility between national policy practices and institutional arrangements, on the one hand, and those applied in the EU, on the other hand. Students of Europeanisation define this incompatibility as 'misfit' that cannot only be found with regard to policies but also in terms of politics, including processes such as interest formation, and aspects of polities such as political institutions or state traditions (Börzel & Risse 2002). A high degree of misfit and limited resources mitigate against both the willingness and the capacity of Eastern neighbourhood countries to engage in policy change (Börzel 2010). However, as Ademmer and Börzel (in this collection) show, a high degree of misfit with regard to policies, politics and polities need not necessarily result in inertia. If the political agenda of the incumbent regime in the Eastern neighbourhood countries is compatible, or fits with EU practices and institutional arrangements, we can speak of a high level of preferential fit that can trigger compliance. Second, since the Eastern neighbourhood countries also lack the prospect of EU membership, the EU's leverage is expected to be too

---

[1]*PCA between the European Communities and their Member States and Ukraine*, 1998, available at: http://me.kmu.gov.ua/file/link/158062/file/ugoda.pdf, accessed 26 September 2011; *PCA between the European Communities and their Member States and Georgia*, 1999, available at: http://mfagov.itdc.ge/files/459_9684_628304_44.pdf, accessed 26 September 2011; *PCA between the European Union and the Republic of Armenia*, available at: http://www.mineconomy.am/files/docs/13_en.pdf, accessed 26 September 2011; *PCA between the European Communities and their Member States and Azerbaijan*, 1999, available at: http://trade.ec.europa.eu/doclib/docs/2004/july/tradoc_116754.pdf, accessed 26 September 2011.

weak to overcome domestic obstacles to change in these countries (Gould 2004; Kelley 2006; Schimmelfennig & Scholtz 2008; Schimmelfennig 2009).

There is no doubt that policy change in the Eastern neighbourhood countries is considerably slower and less comprehensive than in the Central and East European countries. However, recent scholarship has found that the reality is more nuanced than previous discussions have suggested and emphasises variation in policy change across countries and sectors (Lavenex & Schimmelfennig 2009; Gawrich *et al.* 2010; Langbein 2011; Börzel & Pamuk 2012). The contributions to this collection do not only confirm that policy change happens despite high costs, limited capacities and the lack of EU membership prospects. They also challenge some aspects of the conventional wisdom concerning the factors accounting for differential policy change in the Eastern neighbourhood. Finally, our findings point towards important differences between membership, accession and neighbourhood Europeanisation by stressing factors mediating the EU's impact on policy change in the Eastern neighbourhood countries that played a rather marginal role in domestic policy change in EU member states and accession countries.

Policy change despite high misfit and no prospects for EU membership

Despite misfit and the lack of prospects for EU membership, domestic actors in the Eastern neighbourhood countries do not necessarily face higher costs than benefits from the adoption of or behavioural compliance with EU policies. Their incentives and capacities to adopt and implement EU policies vary across policy fields and are not set in stone. Even those domestic actors who have to bear the costs of policy change do not always oppose it. The contributions to this collection show how domestic incentives to demand, adopt or implement EU policies are shaped by a fit with broader political and economic preferences of powerful domestic state and non-state actors or external incentives (policy-specific conditionality such as market access, visa facilitation and financial support). Some of the contributions also emphasise how domestic capacities to make political claims or adopt new policy instruments and implement them are strengthened through technical and financial assistance provided by various external actors, including the EU, international financial institutions or multinational corporations (Ademmer & Börzel; Buzogány; Langbein, all in this collection).

The contributions to this collection reveal that there is not only inertia and resistance but that policy change is rather differential. At times, Eastern neighbourhood countries make only rhetorical commitments to EU policies. At times, they move beyond adopting new laws that correspond to EU policies, which are at least partially implemented by state and non-state actors on the ground, resulting in selective behavioural compliance. Finally, we identify cases where the adopted laws only partially transpose EU rules and are not implemented.

The goal of this collection is not only to show that we can observe policy change in line with EU policies in the first place, but to explain why such convergence varies across policy fields within individual Eastern neighbourhood countries. We will leave aside Belarus since it has not yet agreed on an Action Plan with the EU. Although none of the contributions deals with policy change in Moldova or Azerbaijan, we believe that insights from our case studies also apply to these Eastern neighbourhood countries. As mentioned earlier, we find that broader strategic calculations of powerful domestic actors and policy-specific conditionality or capacity building by external actors shape policy change in Ukraine, Georgia and Armenia. Considering that these policy-specific factors have explanatory power despite different macro-level characteristics of the countries under scrutiny in terms of EU membership aspirations, and asymmetrical interdependencies with the EU or relations with Russia, we can expect similar dynamics in Moldova and Azerbaijan. For reasons of scope, the Mediterranean partners are not included in the analysis either since the 'existence of a more powerful regional track within the Euro–Mediterranean Partnership and of the UNEP-centred Mediterranean Action Plan introduces some institutional particularities' (Costa 2007, p. 2). Finally, the focus on the Eastern neighbours allows us to control for the influence of Russia on policy change in the region. Some scholars consider Russia as a 'regional power that can provide alternative sources of economic, military, and/ or diplomatic support [. . .] thereby mitigating the impact of the Western influence' (Levitsky & Way 2005, p. 9; Dimitrova & Dragneva 2009). Some of the contributions to this collection (Ademmer & Börzel; Langbein) will test this argument.

It is too early to present a consistent theoretical framework to explain differential policy change across policy fields and countries in the EU's Eastern neighbourhood. Rather, the contributions to the collection test tentative explanations that are discussed in the literature and identify explanatory factors for differential policy change that differ from or go beyond insights from the existing literature on membership and accession Europeanisation.

Country-level explanations: membership aspirations and asymmetric interdependencies revisited

The contributions to this collection deal with 'most likely' and 'least likely' cases of policy change among Eastern neighbours. If policy change resulting in compliance and convergence with EU policies is to happen in the Eastern neighbourhood countries, scholars usually expect these changes to take place in Ukraine, Moldova and Georgia. By contrast, Armenia and Azerbaijan are considered as least likely cases (Emerson *et al.* 2007; Franke *et al.* 2010; Gawrich *et al.* 2010). Ukraine, Moldova and Georgia aspire to EU membership. Further, these countries share a relationship of asymmetric interdependence with the EU. In contrast, the relationship between the EU and the other two countries in the Southern Caucasus is more symmetric given Azerbaijan's control over substantial energy resources and Armenia's close relationship with Russia (Börzel 2010).

This collection partly challenges these expectations. Armenia's migration policies increasingly comply with EU demands (Ademmer & Börzel, in this collection). In turn, inertia characterises Ukraine's state-aid policies (Dimitrova & Dragneva, in this collection), whereas there is a great deal of variation within and across various policy fields in Ukraine, including the environment, telecommunications and food safety regulations (Buzogány; Langbein, both in this collection). Our contributions show that policy change can hardly be explained by looking solely at macro-level factors (membership aspirations, asymmetric interdependencies with the EU, etc.). Moreover, we reveal that it is at a policy level that the domestic configuration of actors and their preferences can be fully assessed in the context of non-accession (Langbein 2011; Langbein & Wolczuk 2012).

TABLE 1
OVERVIEW OF POLICY FIELDS AND COUNTRIES COVERED BY THE COLLECTION

	Internal market			
	Economic regulation	Social regulation	Justice and home affairs	Foreign and security policy
Ukraine	Telecommunication and food safety (Langbein)	Environment (Buzogány)		Foreign and security policy (Dimitrova & Dragneva)
	State aid (Dimitrova & Dragneva)			
Southern Caucasus (Armenia and Georgia)		Energy (Ademmer & Börzel)	Migration and anti-corruption (Ademmer & Börzel)	

Policy-type explanations: low politics, high politics and EU-level institutionalisation

Our contributions deal with a variety of policy types covering economic, social and security policies and representing the previous three pillars of the EU: the internal market, foreign and security policy, and justice and home affairs (see Table 1).

In addition, Ademmer and Börzel (in this collection) analyse policy change in areas corresponding to different kinds of EU policymaking, including positive and negative integration (Scharpf 1999, p. 43f.). Positive integration comprises market-shaping policy fields or particular issues that aim at mitigating negative externalities of the market. With its migration or environmental policies the EU prescribes a specific institutional model to which domestic arrangements have to be adjusted. By contrast, negative integration comprises market-making policies that seek to guarantee the functioning of markets through deregulation and liberalisation. This wide range of policy fields under scrutiny allows us to examine to what extent variation in policy change converging with EU rules depends on the type of policy. Early scholarship on European integration predicted more encompassing convergence towards EU policies in technical areas of 'low politics', such as trade-related sectors or the environment, than in the more politicised policy fields of 'high politics', such as energy or foreign and security policy (Haas 1964; Hoffmann 1966). Furthermore, negative integration was not considered as a challenge for domestic policymakers as these market-correcting rules do not force them to build up costly institutional arrangements but rather requires them to abstain from taking actions that would undermine free trade or distort competition (Zürn 1997; Knill & Lenschow 2005). By contrast, compliance in market-shaping policies (positive integration) was expected to produce higher adaptational costs since domestic policymakers must replace their national institutional arrangements in favour of an institutional model prescribed by European legislation. More recent works on the EU's external governance emphasise yet another policy-specific explanation, arguing that EU third countries[2] are more likely to converge and comply with EU policies, the more institutionalised a particular policy field is at the EU level, and the more precise, binding and legitimate respective EU rules are (Lavenex & Schimmelfennig 2009).

However, Dimitrova and Dragneva (in this collection) show that Ukraine's convergence with EU state-aid policies is more limited than with foreign policy despite the fact that state aid

[2]EU third countries are countries that are not EU members or (potential) candidate countries.

is 'low politics' and is more institutionalised on the EU level than the 'high politics' of the Common Foreign and Security Policy (CFSP). Other contributions find significant variation across areas of 'low politics' and highly institutionalised fields, such as telecommunications or food safety (Langbein, in this collection), and across different aspects of the EU's environmental *acquis* (Buzogány, in this collection). In turn, Ademmer and Börzel (in this collection) reveal the impressive record of Georgia in formally adopting and increasingly applying EU energy policies and anti-corruption policies which show similar levels of institutionalisation. Finally, Ademmer and Börzel (in this collection) also show that policy change in the Southern Caucasus does not depend on the market-shaping or market-making character of particular aspects in migration and energy policies.

Formal and informal veto players

Europeanisation in terms of EU membership emphasises the explanatory power of different formally institutionalised veto players that are affected by EU policies in various ways (Knill & Lehmkuhl 2002). The scholarship on enlargement has already shown that informal veto players, such as business actors capturing the state, shape policy change to a larger extent in the new member states than in the old ones since political institutions are often still in flux in the former (Börzel & Sedelmeier 2006). In the Eastern neighbourhood countries, the preferences of powerful business actors play an even stronger role than in the post-communist EU accession countries due to low democratic quality, weak administrative capacities, and prevalent corruption and clientelism (Börzel 2010). Under conditions of poor governance, policy change is most likely where it does not negatively affect the interests of powerful domestic business groups or powerful state authorities which are often backed by economic elites, or where EU policies align with the interests of powerful domestic business groups or political elites backed by economic actors (Buzogány; Dimitrova & Dragneva; Langbein, all in this collection). These interests are not necessarily policy-specific but may be broader in nature, which explains why domestic actors may support convergence towards EU policies despite the high costs involved (Ademmer & Börzel, in this collection).

Policy-specific conditionality and capacity building compared to EU membership conditionality

The contributions to this collection take a fresh look at the mechanisms accounting for convergence and compliance with EU policies in the Eastern neighbourhood countries. In the absence of EU accession conditionality, which has been widely considered to be the key mechanism employed to promote policy change in response to EU demands for convergence during EU enlargement (Schimmelfennig & Sedelmeier 2005; Vachudova 2005), Ademmer and Börzel (in this collection) show that conditionality in the Eastern neighbourhood rather works at the policy level (Langbein 2011; Langbein & Wolczuk 2012). More precisely, the EU mitigates high costs of adaptation for domestic actors in the Eastern neighbourhood countries by tying policy-specific rewards to the fulfilment of EU requirements. This policy-specific conditionality can include market access for trade-related fields, visa facilitation in fields related to justice and home affairs, and financial support that the EU links to domestic reforms in particular policy fields (Buzogány, in this collection). While the application of policy-specific conditionality on its own can at best result in selective or incomplete policy change, it can result in more comprehensive change if the particular EU policy fits the preference of domestic actors (Ademmer & Börzel; Buzogány, both in this collection).

Apart from (policy-specific) conditionality, external actors can empower reform-minded domestic actors by policy-specific capacity building (Buzogány; Langbein, both in this collection). Capacity building can include the provision of financial and technical assistance or the facilitation of lesson-drawing by encouraging domestic participation in transnational regulatory networks.

In sum, the likelihood of policy change resulting in convergence and compliance with EU policies in the Eastern neighbourhood countries increases if external actors apply policy-specific conditionality and capacity building to mitigate adaptational costs and empower domestic actors to advance their claims (Langbein 2011).

The EU and beyond—external actors in the Eastern neighbourhood

Students of the Eastern neighbourhood countries often portray the EU as the key promoter of convergence with EU policies (Lavenex 2008; Wolczuk 2008; Gawrich *et al.* 2010). The contributions to this collection show that the EU is far from being the only, and not necessarily even the most important, external actor that shapes policy change in the Eastern neighbourhood countries. Other international and transnational actors, such as multinational corporations, international organisations, foreign governments or foreign donor organisations, also shape policy change in these countries and contribute to convergence with EU policies. For example, Western European and Russian multinationals investing in Ukraine's telecommunications sector empowered reform-minded domestic state actors and firms by providing financial and technical assistance (Langbein, in this collection). Further, the Armenian diaspora tied financial support to the formal adoption of and behavioural compliance with the EU's anti-corruption policies in Armenia (Ademmer & Börzel, in this collection). Finally, Russian government policies created incentives structures for domestic actors in the Eastern neighbourhood countries to pursue certain policies over others (Ademmer & Börzel; Langbein, both in this collection). Interestingly, at times the EU even undermines convergence with its policies. For example, the highly protected and self-sufficient EU dairy market decreases incentives for Ukrainian dairy producers to invest in local upgrading and to support the application of European food safety standards (Langbein, in this collection).

Russia's ambivalent impact on policy change in the Eastern neighbourhood

In the context of Europeanisation through membership and accession, the EU is the most important influence. Where other external actors, such as international financial institutions, have played a role during enlargement, they have rather reinforced demands of the EU for domestic change by offering additional benefits for the fulfilment of conditions that are similar to EU requirements (Schimmelfennig & Sedelmeier 2005, p. 15). By contrast, the existing literature on the Eastern neighbourhood countries acknowledges Russia as another important regional player shaping policy change in the Eastern neighbourhood countries (Dimitrova & Dragneva 2009; Langbein 2010). It is often argued that Russia thwarts not only democratic development in the region but also the economic integration of the Eastern neighbourhood countries with the EU through regional initiatives aimed at establishing a common economic space among the Commonwealth of Independent States (CIS) or by using (or abusing) economic and security interdependencies (Shapovalova 2006; Sushko 2008; Haukkala 2009; Popescu & Wilson 2009). Yet, these studies remain on a rather general level. They often consider the mere existence of regional initiatives of or interdependencies with Russia as an argument for the countervailing nature of Russia's role in the CIS and treat Russia as a unitary actor that seeks to undermine convergence with EU policies in the region.

Our analytical focus on policy fields brings us to a more refined assessment: rather than treating Russia as a unitary actor, Langbein (in this collection) examines the Russian impact on policy change in the Eastern neighbourhood countries by distinguishing between Russia's political leadership, Russian multinationals and strong economic dependencies on Russia. By doing so, she finds that the Russian impact does not necessarily undermine convergence with EU policies. In fact, the existence of Russia as an additional regional power in the EU's Eastern neighbourhood may both weaken and strengthen domestic support for convergence with EU policies (Ademmer & Börzel, in this collection). For example, where the formal adoption of and behavioural compliance with EU policies by the Eastern neighbourhood countries help Russian investors to counterbalance rent-seeking local elites, Russian multinationals empower domestic reformers favouring convergence with EU policies. At the same time, strong trade linkages between the Eastern neighbourhood countries and Russia may undermine convergence towards EU rules since access to an alternative market reduces the need to adopt and implement European norms and standards (Langbein, in this collection; Dimitrova & Dragneva 2009). Finally, Russian government policies can create incentive structures for domestic actors in the Eastern neighbourhood countries to undermine or facilitate convergence with EU policies (Ademmer & Börzel; Langbein, both in this collection).

The contributions to the collection

The contributions to this collection explore the factors accounting for differential policy change across various policy fields in the EU's Eastern neighbourhood countries and challenge some aspects of the conventional wisdom of the literature on Europeanisation in the EU neighbourhood.

Esther Ademmer and Tanja A. Börzel contradict the widespread assumption that the Eastern neighbourhood countries are the least likely cases for EU-induced policy change due to high policy misfit and the lack of membership conditionality. They argue that preferential fit and policy-specific conditionality account for divergent compliance patterns in anti-corruption, migration and energy policies in Armenia and Georgia. The likelihood of compliance increases if preferences of domestic elites fit EU policies. In the case of preferential misfit, they find non-compliance or inertia. If preferential misfit is counterbalanced by policy-specific conditionality, they find at best shallow compliance. At the same time, relations with Russia can shape EU-induced policy change in the Eastern neighbourhood by creating an incentive structure that mitigates the effects of preferential fit or policy-specific conditionality.

Aron Buzogány's study of change in Ukraine's environmental policy shows that diverse outcomes are possible even within a 'low politics' field. By studying policy change in four sub-fields of environmental policy, he argues that preferences of powerful domestic actors must fit EU policies for the latter to be formally adopted and complied with. In the case of preferential misfit, capacity-building or policy-specific conditionality is needed to mitigate high adaptational costs for powerful domestic actors, but in this case the result, at best, is the formal adoption of EU policies.

Julia Langbein provides a nuanced assessment of the EU and Russian impact on policy change in the Eastern neighbourhood countries. While Russia is widely conceived of as being obstructive to European integration in the Eastern neighbourhood, the EU is portrayed as being the key promoter of convergence with EU policies. By comparing convergence in Ukraine's telecommunications and food safety, she argues that active leverage exerted by Western European and Russian multinationals rather than the EU accounts for divergent outcomes. Furthermore, Russia's negative image does not hold if we stop treating Russia as a unitary actor but distinguish between passive and active leverage exercised by Russian government policies, the Russian market and Russian multinationals investing in Ukraine on domestic policy choices.

Antoaneta Dimitrova and Rilka Dragneva advance an explanation in terms of veto players for the variation in Ukraine's convergence with EU state aid and foreign policies. In contrast to Europeanisation through membership and accession, the presence and actions of informal— rather than formal—veto players significantly shape policy change in the EU's Eastern neighbourhood. Regardless of whether the policy field in question is part of the core EU *acquis* or not, the likelihood of convergence with EU legislation and policies decreases in policy areas where EU rules negatively affect the interests of oligarchs and their political allies.

Freie Universität Berlin

References

Börzel, T. A. (2010) *The Transformative Power of Europe Reloaded. The Limits of External Europeanization*, KFG Working Paper 11 (Berlin, Kolleg-Forschergruppe 'The Transformative Power of Europe', Freie Universität Berlin).

Börzel, T. A. & Pamuk, Y. (2012) 'Pathologies of Europeanization. Fighting Corruption in the Southern Caucusus', *West European Politics*, 35, 1.

Börzel, T. A. & Risse, T. (2002) 'Die Wirkung Internationaler Institutionen: Von der Normanerkennung zur Normeinhaltung', in Jachtenfuchs, M. & Knodt, M. (eds) *Regieren in internationalen Institutionen* (Opladen, Leske + Budrich).

Börzel, T. A. & Sedelmeier, U. (2006) 'The EU Dimension in European Politics', in Heywood, P., Jones, E., Rhodes, M. & Sedelmeier, U. (eds) *Development in European Politics* (Houndmills, Palgrave Macmillan).

Börzel, T. A. & van Hüllen, V. (2005) *Good Governance and Bad Neighbours? The Limits of the Transformative Power of Europe*, KFG Working Paper 35 (Berlin, Kolleg-Forschergruppe 'The Transformative Power of Europe', Freie Universität Berlin).

Costa, O. (2007) *Is ENP Good News for the Transfer of Environmental Norms? Incentives and Socialization for Eastern Neighbours*, Working Paper del Observatorio de Política Exterior Europea 76 (Bellaterra, Institut Universitari d'Estudis Europeus).

Dimitrova, A. & Dragneva, R. (2009) 'Constraining External Governance: Interdependence with Russia and the CIS as Limits to the EU's Rule Transfer in the Ukraine', *Journal of European Public Policy*, 16, 6.

Emerson, M., Noutcheva, G. & Popescu, N. (2007) *European Neighbourhood Policy Two Years on: Time Indeed for an 'ENP plus'*, CEPS Policy Brief 126 (Brussels, Centre for European Policy Studies).

European Commission (2004) *European Neighbourhood Policy Strategy Paper*, COM (2004)373, 12 May (Brussels, European Commission).

European Commission (2008) *Communication from the Commission to the European Parliament and the Council, Eastern Partnership*, COM (2008) 823 final, 3 December (Brussels, European Commission).

Franke, A., Gawrich, A., Melnykovksa, I. & Schweickert, R. (2010) 'The European Union's Relations with Ukraine and Azerbaijan', *Post-Soviet Affairs*, 26, 1.

Gawrich, A., Melnykovska, I. & Schweickert, R. (2010) 'Neighbourhood Europeanization through ENP: The Case of Ukraine', *Journal of Common Market Studies*, 48, 5.

Gould, T. (2004) 'The European Economic Area: A Model for the EU's Neighbourhood Policy?', *Perspectives on European Politics and Societies*, 5, 2.

Haas, E. (1964) *Beyond the Nation-State. Functionalism and International Organization* (Stanford, CA, Stanford University Press).

Haukkala, H. (2009) *From Zero-Sum to Win–Win? The Russian Challenge to the EU's Eastern Neighbourhood Policies*, European Policy Analysis 12 (Stockholm, Swedish Institute for European Policy Studies).

Hoffmann, S. (1966) 'Obstinate or Obsolete? The Fate of the Nation-State and the Case of Western Europe', *Daedalus*, 95, 3.

Kelley, J. (2006) 'New Wine in Old Wineskins: Promoting Political Reforms through the New European Neighbourhood Policy', *Journal of Common Market Studies*, 44, 1.

Knill, C. & Lehmkuhl, D. (2002) 'The National Impact of EU Regulatory Policy: Three Europeanization Mechanisms', *European Journal of Political Research*, 41, 2.

Knill, C. & Lenschow, A. (2005) 'Compliance, Competition, and Communication: Different Approaches to European Governance and their Impact on National Institutions', *Journal of Common Market Studies*, 43, 3.

Langbein, J. (2010) *Patterns of Transnationalization and Regulatory Change beyond the EU. Explaining Cross-Policy Variation in Ukraine*, unpublished PhD dissertation (Florence, European University Institute)

Langbein, J. (2011) *Organizing Regulatory Convergence Outside the EU. Setting Policy-Specific Conditionality and Building Domestic Capacities*, KFG Working Paper 33 (Berlin, Kolleg-Forschergruppe 'The Transformative Power of Europe', Freie Universität Berlin).

Langbein, J. & Wolczuk, K. (2012) 'Convergence without Membership? The Impact of the European Union in the Neighbourhood: Evidence from Ukraine', *Journal of European Public Policy*, 19, 6.

Lavenex, S. (2008) 'A Governance Perspective on the European Neighbourhood Policy: Integration beyond Conditionality?', *Journal of European Public Policy*, 15, 6.

Lavenex, S. & Schimmelfennig, F. (2009) 'EU Rules beyond EU Borders: Theorizing External Governance in European Politics', *Journal of European Public Policy*, 16, 6.

Levitsky, S. & Way, L. (2005) *Linkage versus Leverage: Rethinking the International Dimension of Regime Change* (Syracuse, Campbell Public Affairs Institute, Sawyer Law and Politics Program).

Popescu, N. & Wilson, A. (2009) *The Limits of Enlargement-Lite: European and Russian Power in the Troubled Neighbourhood* (London, European Council on Foreign Relations).

Scharpf, F. W. (1999) *Governing in Europe: Effective and Democratic?* (Oxford & New York, Oxford University Press).

Schimmelfennig, F. (2009) 'Europeanisation beyond Europe', *Living Review on European Governance*, 4, 3.

Schimmelfennig, F. & Scholtz, H. (2008) 'EU Democracy Promotion in the European Neighborhood. Political Conditionality, Economic Development and Transnational Exchange', *European Union Politics*, 9, 2.

Schimmelfennig, F. & Sedelmeier, U. (eds) (2005) *The Europeanization of Central and Eastern Europe* (Ithaca, NY, Cornell University Press).

Shapovalova, N. (2006) *The Russian Federation's Penetration Strategy towards Ukraine* (Toronto, Center for European, Russian, and Eurasian Studies, University of Toronto).

Sushko, O. (2008) *The Impact of Russia on Governance Structures in Ukraine*, Discussion Paper 24 (Bonn, Deutsches Institut für Entwicklungspolitik).

Vachudova, M. (2005) *Europe Undivided: Democracy, Leverage, and Integration after Communism* (Oxford & New York, Oxford University Press).

Wolczuk, K. (2008) *Adjectival Europeanisation? The Impact of the European Neighbourhood Policy on Ukraine*, Global Europe Papers 11 (Bath, Nottingham, University of Bath, University of Nottingham).

Zürn, M. (1997) 'Positives Regieren jenseits des Nationalstaates. Zur Implementation internationaler Umweltregime', *Zeitschrift für Internationale Beziehungen*, 4, 1.

Migration, Energy and Good Governance in the EU's Eastern Neighbourhood

ESTHER ADEMMER & TANJA A. BÖRZEL

Abstract

The literature on European Union enlargement has identified misfit and membership conditionality as two factors that decisively shape the effectiveness of EU policy transfer to the Central and Eastern European accession countries. Thus, European neighbourhood countries would seem to be less likely cases of EU-induced policy change. Yet, rather than inertia or resistance, we find that European neighbourhood countries comply with some but not with other EU policies. Our essay investigates such policy-specific variation in the compliance patterns of Georgia and Armenia that give rise to differential policy change. Comparing the fight against corruption, migration and energy policy, we argue that policy-specific conditionality and preferential fit are the main factors accounting for the EU's differential policy impact in European neighbourhood countries.

THE LACK OF MEMBERSHIP CONDITIONALITY COMBINED WITH a high degree of misfit between EU policies and the domestic structures of European neighbourhood countries have frequently been identified as major constraints on the transfer of EU policies to these countries. Yet, in the Southern Caucasus, we find policy-specific compliance side by side with resistance against EU demands for policy change. Comparing compliance with constitutive, market-making and market-shaping policies in Georgia and Armenia, this essay identifies the interplay of two distinct variables that impact on EU-induced policy change. We argue that policy-specific conditionality and the preferential fit between an EU policy and the political agenda of the respective incumbent elite account for the varying degrees of compliance in the European neighbourhood countries. A high level of policy misfit does not necessarily result in non-compliance, even in the absence of the prospect of EU membership if there is an overall fit between the EU-policy approach and the political agenda of the domestic government. If there is neither policy fit nor preferential fit, but the EU or other international actors invoke high degrees of policy-specific conditionality, we can still expect to see some compliance, which, however, frequently remains shallow and selective.

We illustrate our argument by a comparison of the compliance records of Georgia and Armenia in three areas that are part of the European Neighbourhood Policy (ENP). Our empirical analysis until May 2012 shows that EU anti-corruption policies translate into similar degrees of formal compliance (output) in Georgia and Armenia, whereas behavioural compliance (outcome) varies significantly (for explanations of different forms of compliance, see the Introduction to this collection). The fight against corruption fits the preferences of the Georgian elites and, as a result, formal compliance has also given rise to behavioural changes. In Armenia, by contrast, the high conditionality regarding the fight against corruption exerted by international actors yields only formal changes in anti-corruption policies which have remained largely decoupled from behavioural practices. EU migration rules that are linked to high policy-specific conditionality are equally complied with by both Armenia and Georgia, even though in the case of Georgia behavioural compliance remains shallow due to a high preferential misfit. In the case of energy, finally, which displays only low degrees of conditionality, Georgia complies with market-making policies that fit governmental preferences. Unlike in Armenia, non-compliance or shallow compliance occurs with regard to market-shaping policies that do not fit the preferences of the Georgian government in the respective policy sector.

The conventional wisdom: misfit and membership conditionality

Policy misfit and membership conditionality figure as two crucial conditions that the literature on enlargement and Europeanisation has identified to explain the effectiveness of EU rule transfer to Central and Eastern European accession countries (Börzel & Risse 2003; Schimmelfennig & Sedelmeier 2004). In this vein, if weakly credible or non-credible conditionality combines with high policy misfit or institutional misfit, compliance is less likely to occur because costs are high and the EU offers little to help pay them (Schimmelfennig & Sedelmeier 2004).

In the case of the European neighbourhood countries, the misfit between EU policies and institutional requirements imposes particularly high costs of domestic change. The European neighbourhood countries suffer from serious problems of poor governance, both with regard to effectiveness and democratic legitimacy (Börzel *et al.* 2010b). This is particularly true for the countries and policy areas under scrutiny in this essay. The countries of the Southern Caucasus have so far failed to transform into full democracies and have remained 'stuck' at the stage of semi-democratic or semi-authoritarian regimes in their process of transition. Moreover, they are among the most corrupt countries in the world and lack institutions to fight the massive corruption that prevails in their societies and governments (Börzel *et al.* 2010a). Not only do problems of bad governance leave them far from meeting the political aspects of the Copenhagen Criteria, but Georgia, Armenia and Azerbaijan often do not meet policy-specific requirements for closer political and economic cooperation with the EU either. Prior to the initiation of the ENP in 2003, they had hardly any policies and institutions in place to effectively regulate and govern migration (European Commission 2005a, 2005b; Kabeleova *et al.* 2007). Readmission agreements with the EU had not been put in place before 2006. In a similar vein, the energy sectors of both countries have struggled with underdeveloped infrastructure, little diversification and a lack of market structures, and renewable energies remained underdeveloped prior to the initiation of the ENP (European Commission 2005a, 2005b).

The prospect of EU membership has been identified as a big enough reward to change governmental preferences and balance the costs of overcoming high degrees of misfit in terms of policy, polity or politics (for explanations of different forms of misfit, see the Introduction to this collection). However, even though the European Neighbourhood Policy

(ENP) copies the instruments of enlargement (Kelley 2006), it was explicitly designed without the 'golden carrot' of EU membership. The ENP can only offer specific benefits that are linked to precisely defined steps regarding compliance with certain policies. Such policy-specific conditionality is found, for instance, in the area of migration, where the EU rewards compliance with visa facilitation or liberalisation, or in the reform of internal market rules, which the EU requires before granting additional access to its markets (Gawrich *et al.* 2009; Weber *et al.* 2007).

Since the EU calls for costly policy change in areas as diverse as migration, energy sector reform and the fight against corruption, the prospects of effective compliance would seem to be slight in view of the high level of misfit in all three policy sectors, on the one hand, and the absence of sizeable and credible membership rewards by the EU on the other. However, Georgia and Armenia show similar levels of formal compliance with EU anti-corruption policies, although their behavioural compliance (outcome) varies significantly. Similarly, both countries equally comply with EU migration policies, even though in the case of Georgia, compliance in practice remains shallow. In the case of energy, compliance patterns are even more diverse. While Armenia only manages to comply with market-shaping policies, Georgia shows strong compliance with market-making policies but weak compliance with market-shaping policies. How can we account for such differential compliance in the European neighbourhood countries?

The missing link: preferential misfit and policy-specific conditionality

In this essay we argue that preferential misfit and policy-specific conditionality can account for the differential compliance patterns in the European neighbourhood countries. While we do not deny the importance of policy misfit, it is an institution-focused category that measures the compatibility of EU policies with domestic structures (Gawrich *et al.* 2009, p. 6; Lavenex & Schimmelfennig 2009, p. 805; Mendelski 2009, p. 51), but largely ignores domestic agency and its preferences for change. Focusing on the costs of changing institutionalised practices and rules, this conceptualisation of misfit also ignores the tendency of domestic actors not only to be cost averse, but also to have 'positive' preferences for change in policies and institutions which the EU might empower them to realise. Differential empowerment is a core mechanism or scope condition of Europeanisation and domestic change (Börzel & Risse 2003; Cowles *et al.* 2001; Börzel & Pamuk 2012). However, the EU faces difficulties in empowering reform coalitions that seek to challenge the incumbent government in the European neighbourhood countries as civil society is weak, business is largely co-opted in governmental networks or *vice versa* (Dimitrova & Dragneva, in this collection), and civil and political rights are constrained (Stefes 2006; Stewart 2009, p. 806ff). While non-state actors are incapable and often unwilling to act as change agents, governmental actors can use the EU to push their own political agenda. The use of the EU as an opportunity structure has been amply demonstrated for EU member states and accession countries. In the past, governments have frequently chosen to comply with EU policies in order to be elected or re-elected, or to finance and justify their own policy or institutional preferences (Jacquot & Woll 2003; Woll & Jacquot 2010).

Likewise, compliance with EU policies does not only impose costs for European neighbourhood countries that fall short of democratic standards (Schimmelfennig 2009)—an argument that has fuelled scepticism towards neighbourhood Europeanisation. The policy change requested by the EU can also assist the incumbent regime in gaining and consolidating its power, and may also correlate with the overall governmental agenda or correspond to the preferences of reform-minded governmental actors. We thus define preferential fit as a fit of preferences over policy outcomes. Preferences over outcomes entail the incumbents' intrinsic motivation to maintain or gain political power by improving their position *vis-à-vis* veto players or by advancing their own political agenda. In the case of the fight against corruption, for instance, government actors may prefer to implement EU anti-corruption measures, if ridding the administration of corrupt officials helps to oust political opponents and reward political allies consolidating their grip on power. Such preferential fit can carry considerable explanatory power that might even neutralise the compliance costs caused by policy, polity or politics misfit.

Preferences over outcomes cannot be changed by EU incentives, since the latter aim at altering the cost–benefit calculations for preferences that actors seek to realise and that are exogenous. Preferences over strategies, by contrast, are susceptible to conditionality, by manipulating the strategic choices of actors to comply with externally promoted policies (Frieden 1999). Membership conditionality is certainly a most powerful incentive to change the cost–benefit analysis of candidate countries towards compliance (Schimmelfennig & Sedelmeier 2004). Yet, conditionality might also work at the policy level (Trauner 2009). Policy-specific conditionality is 'weaker' as it does not imply the 'big carrot' of accession to the EU. Rather, it pursues a *quid pro quo* strategy with regard to policy-specific change, for instance by offering market access in exchange for the takeover of EU market rules in the European neighbourhood countries. It targets preferences over strategies, rather than preferences over outcomes, by offering benefits to reduce the costs of compliance or by invoking sanctions to increase the costs of non-compliance. Policy-specific conditionality can be expected to have an enabling impact in cases in which EU demands for domestic change fit governmental preferences and thus allow for their usage. If the policy does not fit the governmental agenda, the high conditionality that is linked to it can change the governmental preferences over strategies without changing the preferences over outcomes. Governmental actors are likely to adopt a policy to avoid potential costs that arise from non-compliance and reap the benefits of compliance. As their preferences over outcomes differ from the EU policy, however, it is likely that the relevant actors only comply selectively or shallowly in order not to thwart their original preferences over outcomes. In other words, policy-specific conditionality changes governmental preferences over strategies rather than outcomes. As we define policy conditionality in terms of rewards or sanctions linked to specific policy reform processes, it is not only the EU that can exert policy-specific conditionality. In cases of institutional strength and governance density in a given policy field (Freyburg *et al.* 2009), it is likely that other international and transnational actors are also equipped with policy leverage. Policy-specific conditionality is thus defined as high if the EU or other international actors explicitly link policy-specific rewards to precise reform steps, and low if they fail to do so.

Recent studies have shown that transgovernmental networks and functional cooperation of different governmental actors may indeed induce socialisation processes altering preferences over outcomes (Freyburg *et al.* 2009; Lavenex & Schimmelfennig 2011). Yet, the functioning of this mechanism presupposes a certain degree of preferential fit in the neighbourhood, as transgovernmental initiatives such as Twinning, the Technical Assistance and Information Exchange instrument (TAIEX) or instruments of legal advice, like the Armenian and Georgian European Policy and Legal Advice Centres (AEPLAC, GEPLAC), are predominantly demand-driven. The respective governmental actors need to consider the EU as a provider of legitimate and effective solutions before they decide to engage in these networks that may then offer additional capacity and empower reform-minded elites.

In order to account for shallow compliance or decoupling effects, we consider two dimensions of our dependent variable. 'Output' compliance relates to the specific political decision or policy adopted by a government (Easton 1957). Unlike 'output', 'outcome' points to changes in the behaviour of relevant target groups causing the problems in the first place (Skjærseth & Wettestad 2002, p. 100). Figure 1 illustrates the compliance tendencies that we expect to emerge from the interplay of our two explanatory variables, 'preferential fit' and 'policy-specific conditionality'.

Preferential fit without policy-specific conditionality produces emerging compliance in the European neighbourhood countries since EU requirements align with the preferences of domestic actors but administrative or financial costs are still high; and since the EU does not provide incentives, domestic actors have to find other ways to pay the costs. Combined with high policy-specific conditionality, preferential fit results in compliance with regard to both output and outcome. In the case of preferential misfit, policy-specific conditionality is still likely to trigger shallow compliance, as the country has an interest in becoming eligible for the provision of incentives from the EU or other external actors, or in avoiding sanctions, respectively, without being willing to implement the rule in practice. In the absence of both preferential fit and policy-specific conditionality, we should expect inertia, as the European neighbourhood countries' governments are unwilling to comply in the first place, nor have any incentive to introduce change (see Buzogány, in this collection).

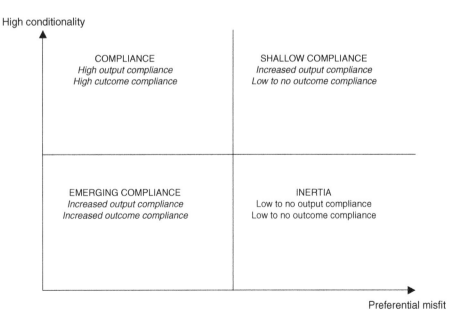

High conditionality

COMPLIANCE
High output compliance
High cutcome compliance

SHALLOW COMPLIANCE
Increased output compliance
Low to no outcome compliance

EMERGING COMPLIANCE
Increased output compliance
Increased outcome compliance

INERTIA
Low to no output compliance
Low to no outcome compliance

Preferential misfit

FIGURE 1. EXPECTED COMPLIANCE TENDENCIES.

Compliance in three distinct areas of ENP

We illustrate our argument by comparing the compliance patterns of Georgia and Armenia with regard to the fight against corruption, migration and energy policy. We focus on compliance with the provisions outlined in the ENP Action Plans as an indicator for EU-induced policy change. We refer to compliance instead of legal approximation or regulatory convergence since the adoption of EU policies does not necessarily result in legal approximation, for example if ENP requirements lack codification, and does not have to trigger convergence with EU rules, as the adoption and implementation of promoted policies might allow for adjusting policies to national peculiarities. Compliance with EU policies and respective policy changes can still result in divergence. For reasons of scope and comparability, we leave out Azerbaijan, as the Azerbaijani bargaining power *vis-à-vis* the EU is significantly stronger compared to Georgia and Armenia due to its wealth in energy resources. This may not only affect patterns of compliance in the energy sector, but in other subfields as well (Börzel *et al.* 2008). The cases we chose vary with regard to both their preferential fit and the degree of policy-specific conditionality.

The three different sectors cover distinct policy types, representing market-making (negative integration), market-shaping (positive integration) and constitutive reforms (for explanations of different forms of integration, see the Introduction to this collection).

Since we compare compliance patterns across these diverse types of policy areas, we also control for their effect on compliance (Knill & Lehmkuhl 1999). Alternative explanations that are covered in the contributions to this special section are taken into consideration. Degrees of codification and institutionalisation are constant across cases. First, we select highly specific policies with similar levels of codification for both countries in their respective Action Plans and international law. Second, we choose countries that participate in the same international fora in the policy sectors under scrutiny in this essay, namely the Budapest and Söderköping process for migration policy, the Council of Europe's 'Group of States against Corruption' (GRECO) for the fight against corruption and the Baku Initiative, the Black Sea Synergy and the Energy Community to which both are observers in relation to energy. Additionally, we incorporate the different forms of transgovernmental networks (Freyburg *et al.* 2009) and touch upon capacity-building measures (Langbein, in this collection) in our analysis. The chosen countries have been eligible for the same forms of capacity building in the framework of various national, regional and thematic ENP programmes as well as for participation in transgovernmental networks, such as TAIEX, Twinning, Support for Improvement of Governance and Management (SIGMA), and diverse legal and technical advice through the respective Armenian or Georgian EU Policy and Legal Advice Centres. As the demand-driven instruments are used differently by governmental actors in various policy fields, this factor is incorporated in our analysis.

The fight against corruption[1]

The fight against corruption figures prominently in the ENP Action Plans. It represents a case of constituent policies that deal with the organisation of political power and require deep and horizontal institutional changes. As regards the ENP, the EU has formulated

---

[1]The empirical data for this section are drawn from (Börzel & Pamuk 2011, 2012) based on a four-year research project (Börzel *et al.* 2009; Börzel *et al.* 2010a, 2010b).

similar demands for the fight against corruption in Georgia and Armenia, causing similar policy and institutional misfit. Yet, despite high costs and a lack of membership conditionality to pay them off, Armenia and Georgia have formally adopted anti-corruption policies (output compliance). In addition, behavioural compliance with anti-corruption policies has witnessed some progress in Georgia (outcome compliance).

EU demands

The EU Action Plans ask the two Caucasian neighbourhood countries to accede to, ratify and implement international conventions that are related to the fight against corruption, including the UN Convention on Corruption, the Council of Europe Criminal and Civil Law Conventions and the Organization for Economic Cooperation and Development (OECD) Convention on Combating Bribery of Foreign Public Officials in International Business Transactions. Georgia and Armenia have agreed to join international anti-corruption networks such as GRECO and implement their recommendations in order to advance legislative or institutional reforms in this regard. Finally, each country has some additional provisions that largely concentrate on promoting anti-corruption measures within the administration or the law enforcement agencies, or improving the legal framework for the prosecution of corruption-related crimes. The required actions are quite similar for the two Southern Caucasus states, and only slightly vary with regard to the specificity of certain measures (Börzel *et al.* 2008). Both Caucasian neighbourhood countries have negotiated with the EU a rather ambitious reform agenda, which constitutes a comprehensive misfit with domestic institutions, policies and political processes.

In the area of the fight against corruption, the application of EU policy-specific conditionality is rather low. Even though the EU has in general the possibility to invoke negative or positive incentives, it has not linked them explicitly to the reform process with regard to the fight against corruption in the framework of the ENP. The Caucasian neighbourhood countries have felt little pressure to engage in domestic reforms to meet ENP goals and requirements, as the EU has almost exclusively relied on capacity building and political dialogue.

Output compliance

Both Caucasian neighbourhood countries have ratified and given effect to the major international conventions on the fight against corruption. In order to abide by their international obligations, the governments of Georgia and Armenia have introduced a number of institutional changes. They have developed anti-corruption strategies and anti-corruption action plans, which are drafted by Anti-Corruption Councils and whose implementation is supervised by special commissions. Moreover, the public prosecutors' offices are charged with the investigation and prosecution of crimes related to corruption. Finally, Georgia and Armenia have introduced several legislative changes by adopting new legislation and amending existing laws (see Table 1).

Overall, the two countries have introduced similar institutions to meet the demands of the EU and other international actors to fight corruption. Given the high policy misfit and lack of membership conditionality, the extent of the domestic changes we observe is not trivial. This is largely explained by preferential fit in the case of Georgia and policy-specific conditionality invoked by actors other than the EU in the case of Armenia.

TABLE 1
FIGHT AGAINST CORRUPTION—DOMESTIC INSTITUTIONAL CHANGE IN THE SOUTHERN CAUCASUS

	Georgia	Armenia
Anti-corruption agencies	Anti-Corruption Policy Coordination Council (2001)	Anti-Corruption Council (2004)
Drafting policies	National Security Council (2005) Inter-Agency Coordination Council of Combating Corruption (2008)	Expert group (2008)
Implementing policies	Department for Coordinating Anti-Corruption Policies (2001) State Minister of Reform (2005) Inter-Agency Coordination Council of Combating Corruption (2008)	Anti-Corruption Strategy Monitoring Commission (2004)
Investigating and prosecution	Prosecutor's Office (2005)	Anti-Corruption Department in Prosecutor-General's Office (2004)
Anti-corruption policies	National Anti-Corruption Strategy (2005, 2010) Action Plan for the Anti-Corruption Strategy (2005–2006)	Anti-Corruption Strategy (2003–2007, 2009–2012) Implementation Action Plan (2003–2007, 2009–2012)
Anti-corruption legal changes (examples)	Amendment of the Criminal Code (2006) Law on Chamber of Control (2008) Amendments to Law on Conflicts of Interest and Corruption in Public Services (2009)	Law on the Office of the Public Prosecutor (2007) Law on Operational Investigative Activities (2007) Law on the Organisation and Implementation of Inspections (2007) Law on the Declaration of Property and Income of Physical Person (2007)

Sources: Börzel & Pamuk (2012, p.87f).

Outcome compliance

Unlike output compliance, the change in behavioural patterns varies between Georgia and Armenia. While levels of corruption have decreased in Georgia, the opposite is true for Armenia (Table 2).

As we will show in the next section, this is less due to diverging EU incentives and more to the different extent to which the fight against corruption fits the preferences of incumbent elites. The Georgian and Armenian governments both engaged in the fight against corruption to ensure and attract foreign aid and foreign direct investments. The Saakashvili regime reportedly used anti-corruption measures to punish political opponents, strengthen the capacity of state institutions and bolster public support. In Armenia, there was no such preferential fit and the Armenian government responded to high policy-specific conditionality mostly emanating from its large diaspora.

In the first decade after its political transition, Georgia had done little to fight the pervasive corruption that crippled its state institutions and its economy (Darchiashvili &

TABLE 2
CORRUPTION IN THE SOUTHERN CAUCASUS

TI Corruption Perception Index		Georgia		Armenia	
Year	Number of Countries Ranked	Score	Rank	Score	Rank
2004	146	2.0	133	3.1	82
2006	163	2.8	99	2.9	93
2008	180	3.9	67	2.9	109
2010	178	3.8	68	2.6	123
2011	183	4.1	64	2.6	129

Note: The scale ranges from 0 (high corruption) to 10 (low corruption). *Source:* Transparency International (2004, 2006, 2008, 2010, 2011).

Nodia 2003; Kikabidze & Losaberidze 2000). President Eduard Shevardnadze depended on clientelistic networks and widespread corruption to consolidate and maintain his power as he lacked the support of a strong and well-organised ruling party (Zürcher & Wheatley 2008; Spirova 2008). Consequently, few changes occurred with regard to the fight against corruption under his presidency. However, Shevardnadze's system of widespread corruption soon became a major point of domestic and international criticism in the early 2000s. As a consequence, the EU restricted its provision of assistance to Georgia in 2003 for the first time (Börzel *et al.* 2010a). In addition, then Minister of Justice, Mikheil Saakashvili, left the government in 2001 and founded the *Ertiani Natsionaluri Modzraoba* (United National Movement), pledging to take issue with the Shevardnadze regime over corruption.

After Shevardnadze had tried to 'steal the vote' in the 2003 elections, mass popular protests and international pressure forced him to resign from office. In the following presidential and parliamentary elections, Mikheil Saakashvili and his party were able to secure the support of large parts of the electorate. Saakashvili declared the fight against corruption to be the core of his government's policies (Wheatley 2005), and was supported by the EU with financial and technical assistance (Börzel *et al.* 2008; European Commission 2011d). The new government immediately took action against corruption within the law enforcement agencies, which resulted in the complete dismantling of the traffic police, which had been considered to be one of the most corrupt institutions in the country. Reforms of the police forces continued with investments in modern equipment, the creation of a new Police Academy, mandatory exams and training for police officers, and considerable increases in salaries. At the same time, draconian fines for minor offences were adopted. Petty corruption was upgraded as a serious crime, warranting several years of imprisonment (Boda & Kakachia 2005; Hiscock 2006).

Saakashvili placed the fight against corruption under the direct control of his government. Since 2006 and 2008, respectively, the Minister of State Reform and the Minister of Justice, who heads the Inter-Agency Coordination Council of Combating Corruption, have been charged with the drafting and implementation of anti-corruption policies. While state authorities targeted petty corruption at lower levels of bureaucracy, Sakaashvili has been accused of turning a blind eye to major corruption and abuse of power among his closest allies, who he himself had allegedly placed in many prominent positions. Thus, corruption has seemingly not been eradicated but rather transformed into elite corruption (Chiabrishvili

2009; Pamuk 2011). As well as rewarding his closest associates, Saakashvili also reportedly used the fight against corruption to oust political opponents (Di Puppo 2009). When the former Minister of Defence and close associate of Saakashvili, Irakli Okruashvili, left the government in 2006, formed the opposition party *Modsraoba Ertiani Sakartwelostwis* (Movement for United Georgia), and accused the president of numerous crimes, he was arrested on corruption charges. A court found him guilty of large-scale extortion and sentenced him to 11 years in prison. What was widely perceived as political persecution sparked mass protests and contributed to the rise of anti-government rallies in 2008 (Freedom House 2008b).

The fight against corruption has not only helped Saakashvili to consolidate the power of his regime; it was also an integral part of the liberal economic reforms of the Saakashvili government. While the Minister of State Reform, Kakha Bendukidze, was proposing privatisation as a major solution to corruption, he claimed that anti-corruption measures promote economic growth by discarding ineffective public institutions (European Stability Initiative 2010). The eradication of entrenched corruption has helped to boost foreign direct investments and economic stabilisation. The EU, the IMF and other international actors, which had suspended assistance before the Rose Revolution, stepped up their financial support for Georgia's new government. The EU almost doubled its support (European Commission 2005b), and the net official development assistance and official aid increased more than ten-fold between 2002 and 2007, as did the foreign direct investments (World Bank 2010). In 2006, the World Bank and the International Finance Corporation declared Georgia the 'top reformer' in the world regarding its business environment (World Bank & International Finance Corporation 2007, p. 1).

In sum, the measures prescribed by the EU to fight against corruption in Georgia fell on fertile ground. The measures helped the Saakashvili regime to successfully break up the informal power structures established by the Shevardnadze regime, to consolidate his new power structures, to step up international support and attract foreign direct investment, and to promote his liberal reform agenda. The better fit of EU demands for good governance and the political preferences of the Georgian government largely explain why Georgia has a much better record of fighting corruption than Armenia. Yet, given remaining levels of elite corruption, Georgia is a case of emerging, not full compliance, which fits our conceptual expectations.

Unlike Georgia, the Armenian government has been subject to high levels of policy-specific conditionality, which, however, do not emanate from the EU, but from other international donors and its diaspora. It has adopted and implemented anti-corruption measures. Yet, corruption has increased rather than decreased (Table 2). This is because the Armenian government has merely used the fight against corruption to deflect international criticism, ensuring external aid and attracting foreign direct investment. Unlike in Georgia, anti-corruption measures have hardly been used to pursue political and economic preferences.

The incumbent regime in Armenia has been rather united and its locus of power has mainly rested with the security apparatus, including the armed forces and related veteran organisations such as the *Yerkrapah*, and with the incumbent *Hayastani Hanrapetakan Kusaktsutyun* (Republican Party) as its political arm (Stefes 2006). In addition, Armenia's historical irredentism, as well as the Karabakh conflict, have created a strong sense of national identity that has bound together the country's various rivalling elite factions and makes them more reluctant to engage in internal power struggles. At the same time, power conflicts have formed along nationalistic issues (concerning Karabakh and Turkey) rather than personal feuds (Hovannisian 2008), which renders the strategic use of anti-corruption measures as a means to consolidate the power basis more difficult. Most importantly, even though the government is characterised by a 'hyper'-executive with far-reaching competences dominating the state apparatus (Shahnazaryan 2003), it largely relies on the support of a wealthy business elite, the Armenian 'oligarchs', as a power base. While the oligarchs enjoy preferential access to the Armenian economy, they reportedly support the incumbent regime, mainly associated with the Republican Party of Armenia, 'helping to rig elections and suppress the opposition' (Danielyan 2006). They have also increasingly assumed membership of parliament (Freedom House 2008a), where they supported the incumbent government, rather than acting as an opposition party (Freedom House 2006). The close ties between political and economic elites are thus both the source of high degrees of corruption (Bertelsmann Stiftung 2010), and the power basis of the incumbent regime. Hence, the Armenian government does not share Georgia's preference for fighting corruption as it poses serious obstacles to maintaining its power rather than helping to consolidate it. Why then did Armenia formally adopt anti-corruption policies in the first place?

The fight against corruption in Armenia has largely constituted a response to the policy-specific conditionality of external donors. Armenia is highly dependent on external financial aid (Libaridian 2004) and suffered a considerable economic setback due to the closure of its borders with Turkey and Azerbaijan in 1994. At the same time, the nationalistic Armenian diaspora is quite influential in domestic politics. Consisting of very disparate groupings, including various organisations and parties in the United States, France and Lebanon, the diaspora provides considerable financial aid and other resources to the country (IOM 2008a; Gillespie & Okruhlik 1991). Furthermore, genuine political parties that enjoy support from influential diaspora organisations have succeeded in building a stronghold in parliament (Dudwick 1993), particularly the *Dashnaktsutyun* (Armenian Revolutionary Federation (ARF-D)) that re-entered the political landscape under President Robert Kocharian in 1998. Yet, corruption and a lack of transparent market rules have been a major impediment for diaspora investors. 'If patriotism helps to buy a ticket to visit Armenia, it is not enough of an argument to part with one's life savings without any guarantee of profit, and without any state protection' (Manaseryan 2004, p. 20). This also holds true, of course, for foreign investors.

In the early 2000s, two developments gave rise to the adoption of steps against corruption in Armenia. First, international donors started to challenge corruption more prominently. The World Bank provided a $345,000 grant to develop an action plan for the fight against corruption, while at the same time officials of both the IMF and the World Bank insisted on its adoption by the end of 2003 (Freedom House 2004). Second, the diaspora voiced concerns and increasingly supported the implementation of domestic reforms of public administration and the judiciary, customs, tax, education, public health and other sectors (Transparency International Armenia 2006). The ARF-D, as the main diaspora-related political organisation, then backed President Kocharian in his campaign for the presidency in 2003, while putting the fight against corruption on their political agenda.[2] It was also the

[2]'ARF to Back Kocharian in 2003 Polls', *AZG Daily*, 2002, available at: http://www.azg.am/EN/2002112601, accessed 12 August 2011.

diaspora-loyal ARF-D that pressed for the establishment of an anti-corruption council, introduced the fight against corruption-related policy changes in parliament and accused Kocharian of protecting big businesses instead of fighting corruption (Danielyan 2004).[3] Under increasing international pressure, the Armenian government made some formal institutional changes and launched publicly visible attempts to crack down on corruption, including the sacking of corrupt officials in the tax department, the customs service and the police. Given their lack of systemic effect, such changes in personnel have been criticised for being merely symbolic (Grigoryan 2008). A similar process marked the aftermath of the presidential elections of 2008, after which Robert Kocharian handed power over to his preferred successor, Serzh Sargsyan. Sargsyan was, similar to his predecessor, renowned for having close ties to the oligarchic business community of Armenia (Freedom House 2004). However, as a reaction to the violent crackdown on protests in the aftermath of the 2008 presidential elections, the US government suspended its assistance to Armenia in the framework of the Millennium Challenge Account programme on the grounds of a lack of democratic governance (Bertelsmann Stiftung 2010). Sargsyan subsequently declared the fight against corruption a priority for his Republican Party. His attempts to tackle corruption, however, have not yet resulted in measurable improvements. Initiatives have only targeted lower governmental levels, leaving the sources of corruption at the top levels of government and business untouched (Grigoryan 2009), and Armenia's corruption score unchanged.

Capacity building can hardly account for the differential compliance of Georgia and Armenia, as Armenia was provided with large amounts of financial and technical assistance in the field of good governance and in the fight against corruption specifically (Börzel *et al.* 2008; European Commission 2011c), which amounted, for instance, to 30% of the overall European Neighbourhood Partnership Instrument (ENPI) budget similar to the amount provided to Georgia from 2007 to 2010 (European Commission 2007b, 2007c, 2011a, 2011b). However, given the fact that Armenia's incumbent elite relied on the root cause of corruption, the symbiosis of economic and political forces, to ensure their political support, capacity building could not balance the costs of fighting corruption for the Armenian government. Targeting primarily financial or administrative burdens, it failed to pay the high political costs for the incumbent regime.

Thus the adoption of formal measures addressing political and administrative corruption in Armenia has been largely symbolic and aimed at placating international donor organisations. Due to preferential misfit alongside high levels of international conditionality, we observe shallow compliance in the case of Armenia and the fight against corruption.

Migration[4]

Reform of the migration policies of Georgia and Armenia has been introduced into the ENP as an instance of 'externalisation' of internal security issues (Di Puppo 2009, p. 106). As the Caucasian neighbourhood countries struggle with problems related to net emigration, the EU hopes to reduce the countries' illegal migration potential by introducing institutional

---

[3] 'ARF Presses Reforms Fight Against Corruption', *Asbarez*, 2003, available at: http://asbarez.com/48744/arf-presses-reforms-fight-against-corruption/, accessed 12 August 2011.

[4] The empirical data the migration and energy sections are drawn from (Ademmer 2011, 2013).

reforms through the ENP framework (Boniface *et al.* 2008, p. 6). Migration reform requires a high degree of regulative policy making and institution building and thus represents market-shaping policies that require the Caucasian neighbourhood countries to engage in positive integration. The EU has formulated similar demands for migration reform in Georgia and Armenia, causing similar policy misfit. Yet, the output and outcome patterns of compliance vary significantly within both countries, as a result of different degrees of preferential fit between EU demands and governmental agendas.

EU demands

The Action Plans foresee policy changes with regard to the security of travel documents and readmission agreements, as well as some policy-specific and institutional requirements related to migration management. More precisely, the EU wants the Caucasian neighbourhood countries to enhance the security standards of passports by equipping them with biometric identifiers. Additionally, it requires readmission agreements that contractually oblige the Caucasian neighbourhood countries to take back migrants illegally residing in the EU (European Commission 2006a, 2006b). Bilateral readmission agreements with individual EU member states had already been requested in the framework of the Partnership and Cooperation Agreement in 1999 (European Union 1999a, 1999b). Institutionally, the ENP Action Plans foresee a strengthening of the capacities of the Migration Agency in Armenia and the Ministry of Refugees and Accommodation in Georgia. In addition, the EU wants the two countries to develop a comprehensive national action plan for migration and asylum issues (European Commission 2006a, 2006b). Unlike in the area of the fight against corruption, or energy policy, the EU links policy-specific, high conditionality to the implementation of the migration management requirements (Trauner & Kruse 2008). These are especially the implementation of readmission agreements and travel document security. The short-term prospect of visa facilitation and the long-term perspective of visa liberalisation are offered by the EU in return. Politically, socially and economically, visa facilitation is deemed highly attractive by the Caucasian neighbourhood countries. It can be presented domestically as a first step forward in the visa relationship with the EU, which is 'felt' in everyday life since visa facilitation makes societal exchange easier and encourages economic interaction for a well-defined group of the countries' citizens. In addition to the overall benefit of visa facilitation, financial support for the reform implementation is provided through the ENPI funding scheme (see Table 3).

Output compliance

As in the case of the fight against corruption, Georgia and Armenia have introduced similar institutional reforms in the area of migration. Even though Armenia can be considered a forerunner with regard to output compliance, Georgia has been catching up. Armenia upgraded its migration institution from an agency to a state committee in 2009 and equipped it with more power within the government of Armenia. Georgia, however, only removed responsibilities for the coordination and formulation of migration policies from its former migration institution, the Ministry of Refugees and Accommodation, and transferred some of them to the more powerful Ministry of Justice in late 2010. Under its auspices, a commission was set up in December 2010 with the task to work on a unified migration

TABLE 3

MIGRATION—DOMESTIC INSTITUTIONAL CHANGE IN THE SOUTHERN CAUCASUS

	Georgia	Armenia
Migration policy	No migration policy document	Migration policy document
Travel documents	Biometric identifiers	Biometric identifiers
Readmission agreements	EC readmission agreement	No EC readmission agreement
Institutional capacities	Set up inter-ministerial working group	Set up inter-ministerial working group
	Downgraded Ministry of Refugees and Accommodation	Upgraded Migration Agency to State Migration Service
	Shifted powers to Ministry of Justice	
Visa-facilitation	Yes	No

Source: Compiled by the authors.

policy (Ministry of Justice of Georgia 2010). Armenia has already approved a 'concept of the state regulation on migration' in December 2010 and passed a national action plan on its implementation in November 2011 (Government of the Republic of Armenia 2011). The draft of a concept paper was created in Georgia in 2008 and an attempt to rework it was started in 2011, but no document has yet been approved by the government. Both Armenia and Georgia completed the technical introduction of biometric passports (Civil Registry Agency Georgia 2011; UNHCR *et al.* 2012), but only Georgia has negotiated a visa-facilitation agreement with the EU (RAPID 2010), whereas Armenia has only been rewarded with the necessary negotiation mandate for the EU in December 2011 and started negotiations in February 2012. In addition, Armenia has not yet signed a readmission agreement with the EU, as Georgia did in 2010, again due to the late provision of a mandate for the conclusion of an overall readmission agreement with the EU in December 2011.

Outcome compliance

Unlike output compliance, outcome compliance differs between Georgia and Armenia. Regardless of the delay of visa-facilitation negotiations with the EU, the behaviour of the Armenian government is broadly consistent with EU policies whereas Georgia only selectively complies. Since policy-specific conditionality is equally high, the variation is to be explained by preferential fit. The EU approach to migration regulation fits the policy preferences of Armenian authorities and equips them with additional capacities to implement their agenda, which results in compliance with ENP policies. In Georgia, by contrast, the ENP migration regime is at odds with the hands-off approach of the domestic government. High preferential misfit combines with strong international conditionalities, resulting in selective and shallow compliance.

Economic considerations have predominantly shaped the non-compliance process in Georgia. The liberal visa regime that the Georgian government designed to attract and facilitate tourism and investments has been a problem for EU officials since the initiation of the ENP. Concerning Georgia's progress in legislative and policy changes in the area of migration, the European Commission's Progress Report in 2008 commented:

Currently Georgia does not have a written migration policy document. [Its] unwritten policy is of an extremely liberal nature and there is no single government body coordinating migration management. Legal provisions regulating the issue of entry into Georgia do not comply with [the] European framework, with a number of significant legislative gaps regarding entry (for example an ordinary visa suits all purposes of entry except for study purposes; irregularities lead only to fines irrespective of length of overstay in Georgia). This is coupled with unregulated labour migration to and from Georgia, leaving room for concern. (European Commission 2008a, p. 8)

Inaction has largely prevailed in policy and institutional reforms since the initiation of the ENP. Georgia's Ministry for Refugees and Accommodation made some use of EU support potentially to implement reforms. It applied for a TAIEX project in the area of labour migration management in 2009 (European Commission 2011d), profited from projects under the EU's thematic programme for migration and asylum, and received support in the framework of the EU-Georgian Mobility Partnership launched in 2009, jointly with other members of the migration commission. This, however, has not yet given rise to policy change. International organisations, non-governmental organisations (NGOs) and EU officials consider the liberal attitude of the government to have caused the prevailing inertia given that the authorities oppose regulation of migration from and to Georgia as an impediment to the freedom of movement. Concerning security-related ENP requirements, Georgia made little reform progress until 2008. Biometric passports were not introduced. Furthermore, negotiations of bilateral readmission agreements had only been successfully completed with three EU member states by 2008 (IOM 2008b, p. 12).

Yet, in 2008, the degree of conditionality applied by the EU significantly changed. Against the background of the illegal provision of Russian passports to Georgians living in the secessionist territories (Goble 2008), the Georgian–Russian conflict and the EU–Russian visa-facilitation agreement, visa facilitation with the EU increased in attractiveness for the Georgian government. While the overall Georgian population still fell under the strict EU visa regime, people in the secessionist territories, who were in the possession of Russian passports, were able to profit from facilitated travel to the EU after the EU–Russia visa-facilitation agreement entered into force. The Georgian government interpreted this as an unacceptable, though unintentional encouragement of separatism (Samadashvili 2007). The issue was increasingly high on the agenda after the conflict in 2008, adding leverage to the European request regarding signing readmission agreements and enhancing document security. Only then did Georgia progress with regard to readmission agreements and document security, which figured as the non-negotiable conditions in the process of visa facilitation in 2008. The financial capacity to implement the document-security reform was primarily provided by the EU (Civil Registry Agency Georgia 2011). The Civil Registry Agency of Georgia was charged with its implementation and managed to introduce the passports in April 2010 (Kirtzkhalia 2010). In reference to the externalities of the EU–Russian visa facilitation (RAPID 2008), the EU and Georgia signed the readmission agreement and Georgia was awarded with a visa-facilitation agreement. Despite the preferential misfit with regard to migration regulation, the additional conditionality imposed by EU–Russian policy externalities triggered compliance in the Georgian case. Yet, the changes remain shallow and restricted to the parts which are directly linked to the EU visa-facilitation conditionality.

The fit between the EU approach on migration and the preferences of the Armenian government can account for compliance in Armenia. The halting of emigration had already figured prominently on the agenda of the Armenian government in 2007 (Government of Armenia 2007). In addition, the intra-governmental competition between the security-oriented police and the management-oriented Migration Service fostered ENP rule adoption. The visa and passport department of the police easily absorbed the request of the EU to implement biometric passports. Armenia started to work on the enhancement of document security as early as 2007 (European Commission 2008b, p. 12). The introduction of biometric identifiers was considered to support the fight against terrorism and to speed up the ENP visa-facilitation process, although the EU had not offered negotiations of a visa-facilitation agreement by that time. The police consequently applied for a TAIEX project to exchange views with European member states on their experience with biometric identifiers in 2007 (Programme Administration Agency 2007). Finally, the issue of biometric passports started in June 2012 on the basis of a presidential decree of 2008 (Government of Armenia 2008). The delay of passport introduction in Armenia as compared to Georgia displays the different forms and extent of EU capacity building in these countries. While the EU issued the first tender for the introduction of passports in Georgia and devoted around €1 million for the required supplies, Armenia received some assistance from the IOM and the OSCE to prepare a tender, but received no financial support with regard to equipment supply. The delay was due to difficult negotiations about the terms and conditions with one of the supply companies.[5] Hence, different forms of capacity building delayed, but did not hamper, the introduction of the new passports in Armenia.

The agenda of the State Migration Service and the EU migration policy converged with regard to less security-driven policy changes. First, Armenia demonstrated its will to cooperate on illegal migration with the EU by concluding bilateral readmission agreements despite the lack of a mandate for an overall EC-readmission agreement. In 2006 Armenia had already finished negotiating bilateral readmission agreements with nine EU member states (Yeganyan 2006). The State Migration Service used the partner country's reintegration assistance that was linked to the agreement to implement its own agenda. With assistance provided by the EU member states, it set up measures to inform potential migrants, prevent second migration and reintegrate returnees. The overall fit of the policy agenda with the EU was also displayed in four TAIEX applications by the State Migration Service to the EU (European Commission 2011c) and a recent Twinning application for the implementation of ENP-related migration policies (European Commission 2011e). The State Migration Service and the police therefore regarded the EU as an opportunity structure to implement their respective agendas, which in the end cumulated in the comprehensive compliance pattern of Armenia in these policy areas.

Energy

Energy policy and energy sector reform is a salient issue in the framework of the ENP, as Georgia has been considered an important transit country for energy reserves in the Caspian Basin. The reform of the energy policies of the Caucasian neighbourhood countries in the

---

[5]'Introduction of E-passports and ID Cards Postponed in Armenia', *Armenian News*, 2011, available at: http://news.am/eng/news/67716.html, accessed 1 August 2011.

framework of the ENP, however, comprises very different approaches ranging from market-making to market-shaping policies. As in the case of the fight against corruption and migration, the EU has formulated similar demands for energy sector reform in Georgia and Armenia, causing a similar policy misfit. Likewise, output compliance and outcome compliance vary significantly within both countries as a result of different degrees of preferential fit between EU demands and governmental agendas.

EU demands

In the energy chapter of the ENP Action Plans, the EU and the Caucasian neighbourhood countries have agreed on specific prescriptions to be domestically implemented. Both countries are expected to strengthen their energy security through the diversification of supply routes and sources, to develop their renewable energy potential and to strengthen the independent regulators on their energy markets (European Commission 2006a, 2006b). The first requirement constitutes a market-making reform, for example by implementing privatisation efforts, breaking up monopolistic market structures and attracting (foreign) investments. The latter requires the countries to shape the market and set up an independent regulatory commission with reference to the EU *acquis* (European Parliament & Council of the EU 2003a, 2003b).

The policy-specific conditionality the EU has attached to these reforms is low. Few project-based conditions are formulated in a very broad manner, such as stressing the respect for democratic principles, human rights and the obligations of the Partnership and Cooperation agreement (European Commission 2004, p. 12). Georgia and Armenia enjoy an observer status in the EU energy community but, as they have not yet applied for membership, this status does not imply a specific conditionality. The overall low degree of conditionality has further decreased since the creation of the Neighbourhood Investment Facility in 2007. With its initiation, EU funding has been explicitly linked to European energy security of supply issues (European Commission 2007a), acknowledging a certain degree of dependence of the EU on Georgia as a transit country. Yet, a high asymmetry in bargaining power favouring the EU has been identified as constitutive for the credible application of conditionality (Schimmelfennig & Sedelmeier 2005, p. 13). In the case of Armenia, only the diversification of energy supply is indirectly tied to a rather high EU conditionality. It is regarded as necessary in order to shut down the outdated Medzamor Nuclear Power Plant, which is located in a seismic zone. The EU has linked the provision of €100 million for the development of alternative energies to the announcement of a binding early decommissioning date by the Armenian authorities (European Commission 2005a).

Output compliance

In the case of market-making regulation, the output performance of both Georgia and Armenia displays similar tendencies. Both countries emphasise energy diversification as a means to establish enhanced energy security in the respective strategic policy documents (Government of Armenia 2005; Parliament of Georgia 2006). In addition, both countries have agreed on gas supply diversification with regional partners. Most importantly, Georgia managed to contractually bind Azerbaijan to gas deliveries in November

2006[6] and in 2008 (European Commission 2008a, 2009). Armenia finalised an agreement with Iran over the construction of an Armenian–Iranian gas pipeline in 2007.[7] Both countries also passed strategies towards developing their own energy resources, mainly hydro-power and renewable energy resources. In Georgia, the main goal of the strategy was to fully satisfy domestic electricity demand from domestic hydro resources (Parliament of Georgia 2006). The Armenian 'Energy Sector Development Strategy' equally stresses the aim to 'maximize [the] use of domestic renewable energy resources for power generation' (Government of Armenia 2005).

The output compliance with regard to the market-shaping policies, however, diverges slightly between the two Southern Caucasian countries. Since 2007, the Georgian National Regulatory Commission (GNERC) has functioned in accordance with the amended 1997 Law on Electricity and Natural Gas (Republic of Georgia 2007). However, the statute of the Independent Regulator leaves some leeway for political interference from the government. Even though financed by the regulated entities, the duties and powers of the commission comprise the 'careful consideration to the main directions of the state energy policy, national security, economic, environmental, and other state policies' and the approval and the dismissal of the commissioners lie with the president (Republic of Georgia 2007, Clause 11.1). With regard to renewable energy development, Georgia does not have a legal framework for promoting the development of renewable energies in place (Energy Efficiency Task Force 2008; INOGATE 2011).[8] Only a purchase guarantee granted by the System Commercial Operator has been initiated as an economic stimulus to renewable energy development. The guarantee, however, provides for the obligatory purchase of electricity produced by hydro-power stations with less than an installed capacity of 100 MW (Government of Georgia 2008b). Yet, only small hydro-power plants, usually defined as stations of 30 MW capacities and less, are considered renewable energy sources due to their small socio-ecological impact (US Department of Energy 2011).

In Armenia a legal framework for the development of renewable resources is in place and comprises diverse regulative measures ranging from laws and action plans to governmental decisions.[9] Furthermore, Armenia also has an economic mechanism in place that is supposed to support financially the development of renewable energies with a capacity of 10 MW and less.[10] The purchase of renewable energy is mandatory at a feed-in tariff of $0.05 per kilowatt-hour (kWh) for 15 years after the granting of the license to the power plant operator (European Bank for Reconstruction and Development 2011).[11] In 2004 the

[6]'Georgian Leader Signals Gas Deal with Azerbaijan', *Civil Georgia*, 2006, available at: http://www.civil.ge/eng/article.php?id=14208, accessed 12 August 2011.

[7]'Iran, Armenia Open Gas Pipeline', *BBC News*, 2007, available at: http://news.bbc.co.uk/2/hi/europe/6466869.stm, accessed 12 August 2011.

[8]'Georgia—Energy Sector Review: Renewable Energy and Energy Efficiency', *INOGATE Energy Portal*, 2011, available at: http://www.inogate.org/index.php?option=com_inogate&view=countrysector&id=19&Itemid=63&lang=en, accessed 12 August 2011.

[9]'Armenia—Energy Sector Review: Renewable Energy', *INOGATE Energy Portal*, 2011, available at: http://www.inogate.org/index.php?option=com_inogate&view=countrysector&id=1&Itemid=63&lang=en, accessed 12 August 2011.

[10]'Renewable Energy Armenia—Hydro Power in Armenia', *Danish Energy Management*, 2011, available at: http://www.renewableenergyarmenia.am/index.php?option=com_content&task=view&id=34&Itemid=113, accessed 12 August 2011.

[11]'Development of Small Hydro Power in Armenia—The Success Story', *Danish Energy Management*, 2011, available at: http://www.renewableenergyarmenia.am/index.php?option=com_content&task=view&id=36&Itemid=114, accessed 12 August 2011.

Republic of Armenia amended a presidential decree of 1997 and regulated the Public Service Regulatory Commission by the law 'On the regulatory body for public services' (Republic of Armenia 2004). Unlike in the case of Georgia, the Commission Statute does not foresee any political considerations to be taken into account by the Commissioners, which formally renders the Regulator more independent of governmental decisions and political interference (Republic of Armenia 2004). As Table 4 shows, the output compliance diverges above all with regard to the market-shaping policy field of renewable energy promotion, in which Armenia outdoes Georgia's compliance record.

Outcome compliance

Unlike output compliance, outcome compliance displays a high variation between the two countries. Whereas Georgia complies with market-making policies *de facto*, Armenia fails to do so, but is a forerunner with regard to market-shaping policies. Since international conditionality is equally low, the divergence in preferential fit accounts again for the high

TABLE 4
ENERGY—DOMESTIC INSTITUTIONAL CHANGE IN THE SOUTHERN CAUCASUS

Policy	Georgia	Armenia
Diversification of supplies	2006: Resolution of the Parliament of Georgia On 'Main Directions of State Policy in the Power Sector of Georgia' 2006: Georgian–Azeri Agreement on gas supply	2005: Energy Sector Development Strategy in the Context of Economic Development in Armenia 2007: Armenian-Iranian gas pipeline operation
Renewable energy	2008: Purchase Guarantee as outlined in the State Program 'Renewable Energy'	2004: The Law of the Republic of Armenia on Energy Saving and Renewable Energy 2005: Energy Sector Development Strategy in the Context of Economic Development of the Republic of Armenia 2007: National Program on Energy Saving and Renewable Energy of the Republic of Armenia 2001: Purchase Guarantee: Decision of the Public Services Regulatory Commission: "Definition of sale tariffs of Electricity Delivered from Plants that Generates Electricity by Utilization of Renewable Energy Resources at the Territory of the Republic of Armenia"
Independent regulator	1997 (amended in 2007): Georgian National Energy Regulatory Commission (GNERC) established by Article 3, Clause 4, Georgian Law on Electricity and Natural Gas	1997: Decree of the President of Armenia 'On the Energy Commission of the Republic of Armenia' (DP-717, April 1997) 2004: Public Service Regulatory Commission (PSRC) established by the Law of the Republic of Armenia on the Regulatory body for Public Services.

Source: Compiled by the authors.

variance in outcome compliance. Being subject to low policy-specific conditionality, Georgia implements an investor-friendly market reform that is in line with the overall ideational disposition of the government, but which constrains market-shaping reforms. The EU approach to positive integration fits the political agenda of the Armenian government. Hence it complies with the EU's market-shaping policies, but fails to do so with market-making reforms.

Georgia managed to *de facto* diversify its resources. Having faced a major energy crisis in 2006, when Russia as the single gas supplier cut its deliveries of cheap energy, Georgia started to do its utmost to achieve energy diversification (Fuller 2007). The provision of technical, economic and political energy security was hitherto introduced as one of the main objectives in the 'Main Directions of State Policy in the Power Sector of Georgia' (Parliament of Georgia 2006). In terms of the development of new sources and routes of supply, the diversification was a success: in 2006, gas was only imported via one pipeline from Russia. Since then pipelines have begun to deliver gas from Azerbaijan to Georgia.

In addition to regional diversification via Azerbaijan, the government put the development of hydro-power resources high on the agenda (Saakashvili 2006). Georgia launched a privatisation campaign in order to boost investment into its hydro-power sector. It introduced a purchase guarantee for power plants sized 100 MW and below, which privileged the development of medium and larger hydro-power stations over the smaller, renewable ones (Government of Georgia 2008b). By these means, Georgia soon managed to cover its own electricity demand with energy generated from its own hydro resources and was even able to export electricity (Government of Georgia 2008a).

Yet, the means to achieve energy diversification were developed against the background of the highly liberal agenda of the Saakashvili government, prioritising market-making over market-shaping measures. The State Policy Framework of 2006 emphasises the 'commercialization of [the] power sector and improvement of its economic situation, with the aim of attracting new investment and development of competitiveness [and] maximum support [for] the activity of local and foreign companies and minimizing bureaucratic mechanisms and procedures' (Parliament of Georgia 2006). The strong deregulation agenda created problems for the implementation of market-shaping reforms, especially as regards the promotion of renewable energy. Renewable energies required the introduction of a regulatory regime to compete with non-renewable energies on a free market (Transparency International Georgia 2008b, p. 13). The lack of such a regime resulted in non-compliance with the ENP prescription of fostering renewable energy development, even though the EU had started to provide for capacities for policy change in this area as early as 1998 (European Commission 1998).

Non-compliance also prevails with regard to Georgia's independent regulator. It does not operate fully independently, but merges with the responsibilities of the Ministry of Energy (Connors & Bjork 2006; Transparency International Georgia 2008a). The increasing control of the independent regulator by the Ministry of Energy can be understood against the background of the highly investor-friendly agenda of the government. Reports of government interference in the activities of the independent regulator have been predominantly connected to the attraction and the finalisation of investment projects. In order to provide attractive opportunity structures such as preferential tariffs to investors that were favoured by the government, the common procedures of the independent regulator were reportedly circumvented and rendered opaque (Transparency International Georgia 2008a, 2008c). The agenda of the Georgian government that comprises investor-friendly and regulation-adverse reforms can thus account for patterns of compliance and non-compliance in the Georgian energy sector in the absence of strong EU policy-specific conditionality.

In comparison to Georgia, the compliance process with the ENP in the energy sector of Armenia displays opposite characteristics. The internal and the external diversification via Iran fits the policy preferences of the Armenian government as displayed in the energy sector development strategy of Armenia (Government of Armenia 2005). The EU welcomed the Iranian–Armenian pipeline construction as a step forward towards energy diversification (Council of the European Union 2007). Yet, unlike what was expected by our model, the preferential fit only results in shallow compliance due to a countervailing incentive structure provided by Russia, Armenia's closest ally in the region. By offering a fixation of gas prices until 2009 and prolonged close energy cooperation, Russia took over 75% of the pipeline and required that the diameter did not exceed a size of 70 cm. Thus, the pipeline was built too small to satisfy Armenian export ambitions (Cheterian 2006). Even though the construction of the pipeline still signifies an infrastructural diversification of gas supply, it did not truly change the supplier dependence, as Russia still controlled large parts of the pipeline (Minassian 2008, p. 8).

The lack of *de facto* diversification severely constrained the possibility of Armenia complying with the early closure of the outdated Medzamor Nuclear Power Plant. Failing to establish an alternative supply regime, the Armenian government refused to give up the nuclear power generation option in 2008 and announced that the NPP will not be shut down prior to its commissioning time.

Unlike its policy of diversification through cooperation with Iran, the early decommissioning of the Medzamor Nuclear Power Plant does not fit with the preferences of the Armenian government. A strongly shared national memory of the Armenian population is linked to the closure of the plant after an earthquake in 1988, which was followed by a severe economic and energy crisis often referred to as 'the dark days'.[12] The Armenian government underlines the lack of legitimacy of the power plant's closure by hinting at international nuclear energy practice as a norm to justify its adherence to the nuclear option. It additionally dismisses public opinion against atomic energy in Germany or France as a temporary phenomenon (Government of Armenia 2005). This resistance has been upheld, despite the fact that the EU has devoted significant financial and administrative support to decommissioning and enhancing the security of the power plant since 1998 (RAPID 1998). The mix of preferential fit and 'cross-conditionality' (Schimmelfennig & Sedelmeier 2004, p. 674) with regard to gas supply diversification and the preferential misfit that manifests itself in the area of the nuclear power plant results in shallow compliance with diversification policies.

However, Armenia fully complies with the renewable energy provisions and has a mainly functioning regulatory commission in place, even though the EU conditionality attached to the reform is rather low. Unlike in the case of Georgia, the independent regulator can be

---

[12]'Kocharian: I do not Rule Out Opportunity of Building New Nuclear Power Plant in Armenia', *Panarmenian*, 2005, available at: http://www.panarmenian.net/eng/news/12773/, accessed 12 August 2011.

TABLE 5
COMPARISON OF TOTAL NON-HYDRO RENEWABLE ELECTRICITY NET GENERATION

Total non-hydro renewable electricity net generation (billion kilowatt-hours)	2006	2007	2008	2009	2010
Georgia	0	0	0	0	0
Armenia	0	0.003	0.002	0.004	0.005

Source: US Energy Information Administration (2011b).

considered to function generally without governmental interference (Sandukhchyan 2006, p. 22). Tariffs follow the agreed methodology and are transparently published by the Commission. Some problems of cross-subsidisation remain, but they are reportedly less related to the overall application of the regulatory framework than to the fact that the wholesale market lacks competing buyers.[13] The Armenian government has also started the development of purely renewable energies, which is very much in line with the attempt to internalise diversification efforts (Government of Armenia 2005). Developing renewable energies fitted all the above preferences of the Ministry of Energy and Natural Resources that applied for a TAIEX project on renewable energy and energy efficiency in 2009 (European Commission 2011c). Unlike Georgia, the Armenian government has not opposed but has welcomed the establishment of a centrally steered regulatory regime for the promotion of renewable energies. It considers the implementation of 'economic and legal mechanisms' (Government of Armenia 2005) important for ensuring the use of domestic and alternative energy sources. As a result, the number of small hydro-power plants, for instance, increased significantly from less than 30 MW of installed capacity in 2006 to 120 MW in 2010.[14] This comparative tendency is also displayed in the development patterns of non-hydroelectric renewable energies in both countries (Table 5).

Unlike in Georgia, the overall implementation of market-shaping EU prescriptions has been facilitated in the Armenian context. This is because the regulatory policy and the strategy of developing the entirety of domestic resources does not encounter any legitimacy problems, but supports the agenda of the Armenian government.

Conclusion

The Europeanisation literature has identified misfit and conditionality as key in explaining compliance with EU demands for convergence or at least alignment with its policies in neighbouring countries. While our policy comparison confirms the importance of these two variables, it calls for a broader conceptualisation. Most EU requirements cause a serious

---

[13]'Armenia—Energy Sector Review: Energy Market', *INOGATE Energy Portal*, 2011, available at: http://www.inogate.org/index.php?option=com_inogate&view=countrysector&id=113&Itemid=63&lang=en, accessed 12 August 2011.

[14]'Development of Small Hydro Power in Armenia—The Success Story', *Danish Energy Management,* 2011, available at: http://www.renewableenergyarmenia.am/index.php?option=com_content&task=view&id=36&Itemid=114, accessed 12 August 2011.

policy misfit and often also an institutional misfit for the Caucasian neighbourhood countries, and the promise of accession without membership probably does not offer sizeable and credible incentives to pay-off the costs of compliance. Yet, misfit does not necessarily result in the rejection of EU policies (Buzogány & Langbein, in this collection). First, the EU's demand for policy change may fit the preferences of incumbent regimes to gain or re-gain political power or push through their own political agenda. Second, the EU (and other external actors) are able to exert significant pressure to reward progress at the policy level. Such policy-specific conditionality becomes particularly relevant when EU policies do not fit the preferences of incumbent regimes. The combination of policy-specific conditionality and preferential misfit results in different patterns of compliance with EU policies.

A preferential fit yields compliance even in the absence of policy-specific conditionality. The EU demands for energy diversification and—to a lesser extent—the fight against corruption became an integral part of the liberal economic reform agenda pursued by the Saakashvili government, which explains why Georgia complies better with these two policies than Armenia despite lower levels of policy-specific conditionality with regard to the fight against corruption. Conversely, preferential misfit most likely produces non-compliance or inertia, unless counterbalanced by policy-specific conditionality, which, however, results at best in shallow compliance as we observe in the case of Armenia's anti-corruption policies.

The only case that is at odds with our model is Armenia's shallow compliance with the EU's demand for energy diversification despite preferential fit. This outlier sheds light on another factor that has been neglected in the literature on neighbourhood Europeanisation. The relationship with Russia may alter the extent to which the EU can successfully induce policy change in its new neighbourhood, mitigating the effects of both policy-specific conditionality and preferential fit (Ademmer 2011, 2013). While the incentive structure offered by Russia has undermined Armenia's compliance with EU-policies on regional energy diversification, this is not always the case (Langbein, in this collection). Thus, the Georgian–Russian conflict and the EU–Russian visa-facilitation agreement reinforced the policy-specific conditionality of the EU for Georgia to engage in visa-facilitation talks with the EU. Likewise, the negative incentives provided to Georgia by Russia during the energy crisis in 2006 figured as an additional stimulus for Georgia's efforts to engage in market-making policies of energy diversification by seeking alternative regional cooperation. Irrespective of the effect on compliance, when the EU is not 'the only game in town', domestic actors appear to have even greater potential to cherry-pick and (ab)use EU demands for policy change to consolidate their power or finance and legitimise their own political agendas.

As this essay goes to press, post-Soviet Georgia has witnessed a peaceful transition of power. With only several weeks in office, Prime Minister Bidzina Ivanishvili's new government has arrested a dozen former officials of the Ministry of Interior on charges ranging from corruption to torture, evidence that may suggest another use of good governance requirements for political purposes. While it is too early to draw final conclusions, further research has to show whether our argument remains valid for post-election Georgia and beyond.

Freie Universität Berlin

References

Ademmer, E. (2011) *You Make Us Do What We Want—The Usage of External Actors and Policy Conditionality in the European Neighborhood*, KFG Working Paper 32 (Berlin, Research College 'The Transformative Power of Europe').

Ademmer, E. (2013) *A Third Rejoices: Russia, the EU, and Policy Transfer to the Post-Soviet Space*, (Phd thesis, Free University of Berlin, January 2013).

Bertelsmann Stiftung (2010) *BTI 2010—Armenia Country Report Bertelsmann Transformation Index* (Gütersloh, Bertelsmann Stiftung).

Boda, J. & Kakachia, K. (2005) 'The Current Status of Police Reform in Georgia', in Cole, E. & Fluri, P. H. (eds) (2005).

Boniface, J., Wesseling, M., O'Connell, K. & Servent, A. R. (2008) *Visa Facilitation versus Tightening of Control—Key Aspects of the ENP* (Brussels, European Parliament—Committee on Foreign Affairs).

Börzel, T. A. & Pamuk, Y. (2011) *Europeanization Subverted? The European Union's Promotion of Good Governance and the Fight against Corruption in the Southern Caucasus*, KFG Working Paper 26 (Berlin, Research College 'The Transformative Power of Europe').

Börzel, T. A. & Pamuk, Y. (2012) 'Pathologies of Europeanization. Fighting Corruption in the Southern Caucasus', *West European Politics*, 35, 1.

Börzel, T. A., Pamuk, Y. & Stahn, A. (2008) *One Size Fits All? The European Union and the Promotion of Good Governance in Its Near Abroad*, SFB-Governance Working Paper 18 (Berlin, Collaborative Research Center 700).

Börzel, T. A., Pamuk, Y. & Stahn, A. (2009) 'Democracy or Stability? EU and US Engagement in the Southern Caucasus', in Magen, A., McFaul, M. & Risse, T. (eds) (2009) *Democracy Promotion in the US and the EU Compared* (Houndmills, Palgrave).

Börzel, T. A., Pamuk, Y. & Stahn, A. (2010a) 'The European Union and its Fight Against Corruption in its Near Abroad. Can it Make a Difference?', *Global Crime*, 11, 2.

Börzel, T. A., Pamuk, Y. & Stahn, A. (2010b) 'Fighting Corruption Abroad. The EU's Good Governance Export', in Wolf, S. & Schmidt-Pfister, D. (eds) (2010) *International Anti-Corruption Regimes in Europe* (Baden-Baden, George C. Marshall European Center for Security Studies).

Börzel, T. A. & Risse, T. (2003) 'Conceptualising the Domestic Impact of Europe', in Featherstone, K. & Radaelli, C. (eds) (2003) *The Politics of Europeanisation* (Oxford, Oxford University Press).

Cheterian, V. (2006) 'Armenien, Iran und die Gaspipeline', *Caucaz Europenews*, 21 May, available at: http://www.caucaz.com/home_de/breve_contenu.php?id=144, accessed 8 March 2011.

Chiabrishvili, M. (2009) 'The Democratic Transformation of Georgia: Independence, Domestic Development and the Secessionist Conflict', in Collmer, S. (ed.) (2009) *From Fragile State to Functioning State: Pathways to Democratic Transformation in a Comparative Perspective* (Berlin, George C. Marshall European Center for Security Studies).

Civil Registry Agency Georgia (2011) 'The First Biometric Passport was Issued in Georgia', 15 April, available at: http://www.cra.gov.ge/index.php?lang_id=ENG&sec_id=49&info_id=1245, accessed 13 May 2012.

Cole, E. & Fluri, P. H. (eds) (2005) *From Revolution to Reform. Georgia's Struggle with Democratic Institution Building and Security Sector Reform* (Geneva, Geneva Centre for the Democratic Control of Armed Forces (DCAF)).

Connors, C. R. & Bjork, I. M. (2006) *Georgia: Report on the Status of GNERC* (Washington, DC, USAID, Pierce Atwood).

Cowles, M. G., Caporaso, J. A. & Risse, T. (2001) *Transforming Europe. Europeanization and Domestic Change* (Ithaca, NY, Cornell University Press).

Council of the European Union (2007) *Note from the General Secretariat of the Council to Delegations, Ninth Meeting of EU-Armenia Parliamentary Cooperation Committee*, 6247/07, adopted 12 February 2007, (Brussels, Council of the European Union).

Danielyan, E. (2004) 'Armenia's Ruling Coalition Beset by Renewed Infighting', 12 February, available at: http://www.eurasianet.org/departments/insight/articles/eav021304.shtml, accessed 13 May 2012.

Danielyan, E. (2006) 'Armenian Oligarch Makes Bid for Power with New Political Party', 13 January, available at: http://www.jamestown.org/single/?no_cache=1&tx_ttnews[tt_news]=31284, accessed 13 May 2012.

Darchiashvili, D. & Nodia, G. (2003) *Building Democracy in Georgia: Power Structures, the Weak State Syndrome and Corruption*, Discussion Paper 5 (Stockholm, International Institute for Democracy and Electoral Assistance).

Di Puppo, L. (2009) 'The Externalization of JHA Policies in Georgia: Partner or Hotbed of Threats?', *Journal of European Integration*, 31, 1.

Dudwick, N. (1993) 'Armenia: The Nation Awakens', in Bremmer, I. & Taras, R. (eds) (1993) *Nation and Politics in the Soviet Successor States* (New York, Cambridge University Press).

Easton, D. (1957) 'An Approach to the Analysis of Political Systems', *World Politics*, 9, 3.

Energy Efficiency Task Force (2008) *Report on Energy Efficiency in the Contracting Parties and Observer Countries to the Treaty Establishing the Energy Community* (Vienna, Energy Community).

European Bank for Reconstruction and Development (EBRD) (2011) 'Renewable Development Initiative: Armenia—Country Profile', available at: http://www.ebrdrenewables.com/sites/renew/countries/Armenia/default.aspx, accessed 12 August 2011.

European Commission (1998) *Bericht der Kommission—TACIS Jahresbericht 1998* (Brussels, European Commission).

European Commission (2004) *TACIS Regional Action Programme 2004 Regulation* (Brussels, European Commission).

European Commission (2005a) *European Neighbourhood Policy—Country Report Armenia Communities* (Brussels, European Commission).

European Commission (2005b) *European Neighbourhood Policy—Country Report Georgia Communities* (Brussels, European Commission).

European Commission (2006a) *EU/Georgia Action Plan* (Brussels, European Commission).

European Commission (2006b) *EU/Armenia Action Plan* (Brussels, European Commission).

European Commission (2007a) *European Neighbourhood and Partnership Instrument—Georgia—Country Strategy Paper 2007–2013 Main* (Brussels, European Commission).

European Commission (2007b) *European Neighbourhood and Partnership Instrument Armenia: National Indicative Programme 2007–2010* (Brussels, European Commission).

European Commission (2007c) *European Neighbourhood and Partnership Instrument Georgia: National Indicative Programme 2007–2010* (Brussels, European Commission).

European Commission (2008a) *Communication from the Commission to the Council and the European Parliament 'Implementation of the European Neighbourhood Policy in 2007' Progress Report Georgia* (Brussels, European Commission).

European Commission (2008b) *Communication from the Commission to the Council and the European Parliament 'Implementation of the European Neighbourhood Policy in 2007' Progress Report Armenia* (Brussels, European Commission).

European Commission (2009) *Communication from the Commission to the Council and the European Parliament 'Implementation of the European Neighbourhood Policy in 2008' Progress Report Georgia Policy* (Brussels, European Commission).

European Commission (2011a) *European Neighbourhood and Partnership Instrument Armenia: National Indicative Programme 2007–2010* (Brussels, European Commission).

European Commission (2011b) *European Neighbourhood and Partnership Instrument Georgia: National Indicative Programme 2007–2010* (Brussels, European Commission).

European Commission (2011c) 'TAIEX Events Library—"Location: Armenia"', available at: http://ec.europa.eu/enlargement/taiex/dyn/taiex-events/index_en.jsp, accessed 12 August 2011.

European Commission (2011d) 'TAIEX Events Library—"Location: Georgia"', available at: http://ec.europa.eu/enlargement/taiex/dyn/taiex-events/index_en.jsp, accessed 12 August 2011.

European Commission (2011e) *Twinning News 22. Boosting Co-operation through Twinning* (Brussels, European Commission).

European Parliament & Council of the EU (2003a) 'Directive 2003/54/EC of 26 June 2003 Concerning Common Rules for the Internal Market in Electricity and Repealing Directive 96/92/EC', *Official Journal of the European Union*, L 176/37 (Brussels).

European Parliament & Council of the EU (2003b) 'Directive 2003/55/EC of 26 June 2003 Concerning Common Rules for the Internal Market in Natural Gas and Repealing Directive 98/30/EC', *Official Journal of the European Union*, L 176/57 (Brussels).

European Stability Initiative (2010) *Part III: Jacobins in Tbilisi Georgia's Libertarian Revolution* (Berlin, Tbilisi & Istanbul, European Stability Initiative).

European Union (1999a) *Partnership and Cooperation Agreement between the European Communities and their Member States, of the One Part, and Armenia, of the Other Part* (Brussels, European Commission).

European Union (1999b) *Partnership and Cooperation Agreement between the European Communities and their Member States, of the One Part, and Georgia, of the Other Part* (Brussels, European Commission).

Freedom House (2004) *Country Report—Armenia Countries at the Crossroads 2004* (Washington, DC, Freedom House).

Freedom House (2006) *Country Report—Armenia Countries at the Crossroads* (Washington, DC, Freedom House).

Freedom House (2007) *Nations in Transit—Country Report Georgia* (Washington, DC, Freedom House).

Freedom House (2008a) *Nations in Transit—Country Report Armenia* (Washington, DC, Freedom House).

Freedom House (2008b) *Nations in Transit—Country Report Georgia* (Washington, DC, Freedom House).

Freyburg, T., Lavenex, S., Schimmelfennig, F., Skripka, T. & Wetzel, A. (2009) 'EU Promotion of Democratic Governance in the Neighbourhood', *Journal of European Public Policy*, 16, 6.

Frieden, J. (1999) 'Actors and Preferences in International Relations', in Lake, D. A. & Powell, R. (eds) (1999) *Strategic Choice and International Relations* (Princeton, NJ, Princeton University Press).

Fuller, L. (2007) 'Caucasus: Georgia, Azerbaijan Seek Alternatives to Russian Gas', *Radio Free Europe/Radio Liberty*, 5 January.

Gawrich, A., Melnykovska, I. & Schweickert, R. (2009) *Neighbourhood Europeanization through ENP: The Case of Ukraine*, KFG Working Paper 3 (Berlin, Research College 'The Transformative Power of Europe').

Gillespie, K. & Okruhlik, G. (1991) 'The Political Dimensions of Corruption Cleanups: A Framework for Analysis', *Comparative Politics*, 24, 1.

Goble, P. A. (2008) 'Russian "Passportization"', *The New York Times*, 9 September.

Government of Armenia (2005) *Energy Sector Development Strategy in the Context of Economic Development in Armenia* (Yerevan, Government of Armenia).

Government of Armenia (2007) *Republic of Armenia Government Program—Statement by RA Prime Minister Serzh Sargsyan in RA National Assembly at Presentation of RA Government Program Assembly* (Yerevan, Government of Armenia).

Government of Armenia (2008) *Decree N 380-A on Republic of Armenia Government Program* (Yerevan, Government of Armenia).

Government of Georgia (2008a) *Overview of the Georgian Electricity Sector, Provided by: Nana Pirtskhelani, Deputy Head of International Relations and Investment Project Department in the Ministry of Energy of Georgia on 21.06.2008* (Tbilisi, Government of Georgia).

Government of Georgia (2008b) *State Program 'Renewable Energy 2008'—Rule on the Construction of the New Renewable Energy Sources in Georgia* (Tbilisi, Government of Georgia).

Government of the Republic of Armenia (2011) *Decision N1593-N on Approving the '2012–2016 Action Plan for Implementation of the Concept for the Policy of State Regulation of Migration in the Republic of Armenia'* (Yerevan, Government of Armenia).

Grigoryan, M. (2008) 'Armenia: Getting Serious About Corruption', 10 July 2008, available at: http://www.eurasianet.org/departments/insight/articles/eav071108.shtml, accessed 16 May 2012.

Grigoryan, M. (2009) 'Armenia: Yerevan's Anti-Corruption Campaign Going Nowhere Fast—Experts', 8 December, available at: http://www.eurasianet.org/departments/insight/articles/eav120909a.shtml, accessed 13 May 2012.

Hiscock, D. (2006) 'The Commercialisation of Post-Soviet Private Security', in Cole, E. & Fluri, P. H. (eds) (2006).

Hovannisian, R. K. (2008) *Forward to the Past: Russia, Turkey, and Armenia's Fate* (Yerevan, Armenian Center for National and International Studies (ACNIS)).

INOGATE (2011) 'Georgia—Energy Sector Review: Renewable Energy and Energy Efficiency', available at: http://www.inogate.org/index.php?option=com_inogate&view=countrysector&id=19&Itemid=63&lang=en, accessed 12 August 2011.

IOM (2008a) *Migration in Armenia. A County Profile 2008* (Geneva, International Organization for Migration).

IOM (2008b) *Review of Migration Management in Georgia—Assessment Mission Report* (Tbilisi, International Organization for Migration).

Jacquot, S. & Woll, C. (2003) 'Usage of European Integration—Europeanisation from a Sociological Perspective', *European Integration Online Papers*, 7, 12.

Kabeleova, H., Mazmanyan, A. & Yeremyan, A. (2007) *Assessment of the Migration Legislation in the Republic of Armenia* (Yerevan, OSCE).

Kelley, J. (2006) 'New Wine in Old Wineskins: Promoting Political Reforms through the New European Neighbourhood Policy', *Journal of Common Market Studies*, 44, 1.

Kikabidze, K. & Losaberidze, D. (2000) *Institutionalism and Clientelism in Georgia* (Tbilisi, NEKERI).

Kirtzkhalia, N. (2010) 'Georgia Will Issue Biometric Passports Today', available at: http://en.trend.az/regions/scaucasus/georgia/1669937.html, accessed 12 August 2011.

Knill, C. & Lehmkuhl, D. (1999) 'How Europe Matters. Different Mechanisms of Europeanization', *European Integration Online Papers*, 3, 7.

Lavenex, S. & Schimmelfennig, F. (2009) 'EU Rules Beyond EU Borders: Theorizing External Governance in European Politics', *Journal of European Public Policy*, 16, 6.

Lavenex, S. & Schimmelfennig, F. (2011) 'EU democracy promotion in the neighbourhood: from leverage to governance', *Democratization*, 18, 4.

Libaridian, G. J. (2004) *Modern Armenia: People, Nation, State* (New Brunswick, NJ, Transaction Publishers).

Manaseryan, T. (2004) *Diaspora: The Comparative Advantage for Armenia* (Washington, DC, Yerevan, Armenian International Policy Research Group).

Mendelski, M. (2009) 'The Impact of the EU on Governance Reforms in Post-Communist Europe: A Comparison between First and Second-Wave Candidates', *Romanian Journal of Political Science*, 9, 2.

Migration Agency of the RA Ministry of Territorial Administration (2010) *Discussions of the National Draft Program on Migration and Asylum, February 24* (Yerevan, Ministry of Territorial Administration).

Minassian, G. (2008) *Armenia, a Russian Outpost in the Caucasus?* Russie.Nei.Visions 27 (Paris, Institut français des relations internationales).

Ministry of Justice of Georgia (2010) *First Session of State Commission on Migration Issues was Held at Ministry of Justice of Georgia* (Tbilisi, Ministry of Justice of Georgia).

Pamuk, Y. (2011) *Wandel und Kontinuität—Acht Jahre nach der Rosenrevolution in Georgien*, Hintergrundpapier No. 13 (Tbilisi, Friedrich Naumann Stiftung für die Freiheit).

Panarmenian.net (2011) 'Biometric Passport to Cost AMD 1000', available at: http://www.panarmenian.net/eng/society/news/59707/, accessed 12 August 2011.

Parliament of Georgia (2006) *Resolution of the Parliament of Georgia on 'Main Directions of State Policy in the Power Sector of Georgia'* (Tbilisi, Parliament of Georgia).

Programme Administration Agency (2007) *TAIEX Events for 2007* (Yerevan, Ministry of Economy of the Republic of Armenia) available at: http://www.pao-armenia.am/en/taiex_pline/, accessed 12 August 2011.

RAPID (1998) *EU Grants Armenia an Exceptional Financial Assistance*, Europa Press Releases (Brussels, European Commission).

RAPID (2008) *Commission Recommends the Negotiation of Visa Facilitation and Readmission Agreements with Georgia*, Europa Press Releases (Brussels, European Commission).

RAPID (2010) *The EU Strengthens Visa Cooperation with Georgia*, Europa Press Releases (Brussels, European Commission).

Republic of Armenia (2004) *The Law of the Republic of Armenia On the Regulatory Body for Public Services* (Yerevan, Public Services Regulatory Commission of the Republic of Armenia).

Republic of Georgia (2007) *Georgian Law on Electricity and Natural Gas Distribution* (Tbilisi, Georgian National Energy and Water Supply Regulatory Commission).

Saakashvili, M. (2006) 'President Saakashvili Holds Energy Commission Meeting', 25 April, available at: http://www.president.gov.ge/index.php?lang_id=ENG&sec_id=228&info_id=4780, accessed 15 June 2010.

Samadashvili, S. (2007) 'EU Visa Policy Endangers Georgia Peace Effort', *EU Observer*, 12 June.

Sandukhchyan, D. (2006) *Armenia. Final Report: Monitoring of Russia and Ukraine (Priority 1) and Armenia, Azerbaijan, Belarus, Georgia, Kazakhstan and Moldova (Priority 2): Telecommunications and the Information Society* (Brussels, European Commission).

Schimmelfennig, F. (2009) 'Europeanization beyond Europe', *Living Reviews in European Governance*, 4, 3.

Schimmelfennig, F. & Sedelmeier, U. (2004) 'Governance by Conditionality: EU Rule Transfer to the Candidate Countries of Central and Eastern Europe', *Journal of European Public Policy*, 11, 4.

Schimmelfennig, F. & Sedelmeier, U. (2005) *The Europeanization of Central and Eastern Europe* (Ithaca, NY, Cornell University Press).

Shahnazaryan, N. (2003) *Oligarchs in Armenia* (Yerevan, Armenia—Business and Legal Advisors and Auditors).

Skjærseth, J. B. & Wettestad, J. (2002) 'Understanding the Effectiveness of EU Environmental Policy: How Can Regime Analysis Contribute?', *Environmental Politics*, 11, 3.

Spirova, M. (2008) 'Corruption and Democracy—The "Color Revolutions" in Georgia and Ukraine', *Taiwan Journal of Democracy*, 4, 2.

Stefes, C. H. (2006) *Understanding Post-Soviet Transitions—Corruption, Collusion and Clientelism* (Basingstoke, Palgrave).

Stewart, S. (2009) 'The Interplay of Domestic Contexts and External Democracy Promotion: Lessons from Eastern Europe and the South Caucasus', *Democratization*, 16, 4.

Transparency International (2004) 'Corruption Perceptions Index 2004', available at: http://www.transparency.org/policy_research/surveys_indices/cpi, accessed 6 June 2011.

Transparency International (2006) 'Corruption Perceptions Index 2006', available at: http://www.transparency.org/policy_research/surveys_indices/cpi, accessed 6 June 2011.

Transparency International (2008) 'Corruption Perceptions Index 2008', available at: http://www.transparency.org/policy_research/surveys_indices/cpi, accessed 6 June 2011.

Transparency International (2010) 'Corruption Perceptions Index 2010', available at: http://www.transparency.org/policy_research/surveys_indices/cpi, accessed 6 June 2011.

Transparency International (2011) 'Corruption Perceptions Index 2011', available at: http://cpi.transparency.org/cpi2011/results/, accessed 16 May 2012.

Transparency International Armenia (2006) *Anti-Corruption Policy in Armenia* (Yerevan, Transparency International Armenia).

Transparency International Georgia (2008a) *Georgia's State Policy in the Electricity Sector Brief History and Ongoing Processes* (Tbilisi, Transparency International Georgia).

Transparency International Georgia (2008b) *National Policy of Georgia on Developing Renewable Energy Sources Energy* (Tbilisi, Transparency International Georgia).

Transparency International Georgia (2008c) *State Policies of Georgia in the Energy Sector: Tariffs on Electricity and Gas October* (Tbilisi, Transparency International Georgia).

Trauner, F. (2009) 'From Membership Conditionality to Policy Conditionality: EU External Governance in South Eastern Europe', *Journal of European Public Policy*, 16, 5.

Trauner, F. & Kruse, I. (2008) 'EC Visa Facilitation and Readmission Agreements: A New Standard EU Foreign Policy Tool?', *European Journal of Migration and Law*, 10, 4.

UNHCR, Migrationsverket & IOM (2012) 'Armenia to Switch to Biometric Passports in June', 4 February, available at: http://soderkoping.org.ua/page36878.html, accessed 13 May 2012.

US Department of Energy (2011) *Large-Scale Hydropower Energy Basics* (Washington, DC, US Department of Energy).

US Energy Information Administration (2011a) *International Energy Statistics—Total Electricity Net Generation* (Washington, DC, US Department of Energy) available at: http://www.eia.gov/cfapps/ipdbproject/iedindex3.cfm?tid=2&pid=2&aid=12&cid=AM,GG,&syid=2006&eyid=2009&unit=BKWH, accessed 6 June 2011.

US Energy Information Administration (2011b) *International Energy Statistics—Total Non-Hydro Renewable Electricity Net Generation* (Washington, DC, US Department of Energy) available at: http://www.eia.gov/cfapps/ipdbproject/iedindex3.cfm?tid=2&pid=34&aid=12&cid=AM,GG,&syid=2005&eyid=2009&unit=BKWH, accessed 6 June 2011.

Weber, K., Smith, M. E. & Baun, M. (eds) (2007) *Governing Europe's Neighbourhood: Partners or Periphery?* (Manchester, Manchester University Press).

Wheatley, J. (2005) *Georgia from National Awakening to Rose Revolution. Delayed Transition in the Former Soviet Union* (Aldershot, Ashgate).

Woll, C. & Jacquot, S. (2010) 'Using Europe: Strategic Action in Multi-Level Politics', *Comparative European Politics*, 8, 1.

World Bank (2010) *World DataBank* (Washington, DC, World Bank).

World Bank & International Finance Corporation (2007) *Doing Business 2007: How To Reform* (Washington, DC, World Bank, International Finance Corporation).

Yeganyan, G. (2006) *Statement of Mr. Gagik Yeganyan, Head of Migration Agency, Ministry of Territorial Administration of the Republic of Armenia Cluster Process Meeting—European and Southern Caucasus Countries: Topic IV: Readmission Agreements* (Yerevan, Ministry of Territorial Administration of the Republic of Armenia).

Zürcher, C. & Wheatley, J. (2008) 'On the Origin and Consolidation of Hybrid Regimes. The State of Democracy in the Caucasus', *Taiwan Journal of Democracy*, 4, 1.

Selective Adoption of EU Environmental Norms in Ukraine. Convergence *á la Carte*

ARON BUZOGÁNY

Abstract

While the EU's policies towards non-member states are often discussed within frameworks of 'high politics', one of the most important features of the European Neighbourhood Policy is its emphasis on the 'low politics' of sectoral dialogue in functionally differentiated policy fields. Examining policy change triggered in Ukraine by the EU's neighbourhood policy framework, the essay focuses on environmental policy as a typical 'low politics' policy field. The results show that in four sub-fields of environmental policy case-specific constellations of domestic veto players, policy-specific conditionality and external capacity building determine domestic policy change.

ONE OF THE MOST SALIENT CONCERNS OF THE EU's external governance is to induce policy change abroad. This has been a highly successful strategy in cases where new countries, such as the Central and East European states, were subsequently granted EU membership. Without the promise of membership however, most policy makers and policy analysts share a great deal of scepticism about the prospects of externally induced policy change (Börzel 2010). The main reason for such scepticism is that without the prospect of membership, conditionality cannot be used to override the high domestic costs caused by adopting EU norms. However, others argue on a more optimistic note that the transformative power of the EU is not necessarily doomed to fail because of the lack of prospects of membership (Lavenex & Wichmann 2009). Alternative mechanisms of EU external rule projection can rely on international treaties (Barbé *et al.* 2009), make use of market access or visa issues as leverage over governments (Vachudová 2007; Langbein 2010a),[1] or promote capacity building and socialisation in administrative, business or civil society networks (Freyburg *et al.* 2009).

This latter perspective is closely related to scholarship on interdependence in international political economy (Keohane & Nye 1989) and neo-functionalist reasoning on EU integration, which stood at the core of the so-called Monnet method of '*petits pas, grands effets*'. As Haas and Lindberg argued, flows of trade and investments across national

The author would like to thank the two anonymous referees, as well as Tanja Börzel and Julia Langbein for their helpful comments.

[1]See also Ademmer and Börzel, in this collection.

borders, together with technocratic and technical regulations made necessary by such movements, were among the main drivers of European integration in the 1950s (Lindberg 1963; Haas 1964). They also highlighted the role of 'spill-overs' from depoliticised sectors characterised by 'low politics' into other policy areas. More than 50 years later, this logic seems not to be restricted to member states, but to apply also in countries beyond the EU's borders. While the EU has been rather reluctant—or unable—to solve 'hard' security issues such as territorial conflicts in its neighbourhood countries (Popescu 2010), it seeks actively to encourage domestic reforms through 'external governance' which rely on the 'export' of EU standards and norms (Lavenex 2004; Lavenex & Schimmelfennig 2009; Friis & Murphy 1999; Freyburg *et al.* 2009).

Conceptualisations of external governance usually start with the perception of the EU as a dynamic multi-level governance system, characterised by continuity between internal and external developments in the policy process (Christiansen *et al.* 2000). This perspective is particularly helpful for analysing cooperative relations beneath the threshold of EU membership as it focuses on the transmission of EU policies beyond its territory. However, recent scholarship on norm transfer in the European Neighbourhood Policy (ENP) framework has been mostly concerned with external factors driving policy change towards the EU. Several assumptions, mostly implicit, and rarely explicit, have underpinned this choice. One assumption was that the EU's neighbourhood countries are akin to the Central and East European states in their unconditional digestion of the EU's *acquis* without considering domestic costs. This implied also that political parties and public opinion in these countries on the periphery of the EU would recognise and follow the EU as an unequivocal 'force for good' (Barbé & Johansson-Nogués 2008, p. 81). However, a closer look at the ENP countries allows questioning some of these commonly held assumptions. As Dimitrova and Dragneva (2009) have shown for Ukraine, the EU is not necessarily the only central policy actor affecting domestic policy makers. Even Ukraine, for a long time an ardent supporter of convergence with EU norms, has recognised in its implementation strategy that adoption of EU law is conditional on its political, economic and social appropriateness (Albi 2009). A second questionable assumption has been to take for granted the EU's rhetoric about the 'shared ownership' character of the goals agreed in the Action Plans. In fact, such 'shared goals' are more likely to be the results of bargains and package deals between the EU and domestic actors and this can considerably reduce the likelihood of norm and rule adoption resulting in policy change (Casier 2011). Finally, relatively little attention has been paid to sectoral or sub-sectoral differences in convergence with EU norms. While according to an evaluation by a Ukrainian think-tank, 224 of 227 government reforms were in line with the Action Plan in 2007 (Melnykovska & Schweickert 2008, p. 22), the levels of implementation are perhaps more telling: only one third of these reforms could be considered 'fully implemented'. The same evaluation also found substantial differences between policy fields, as 'almost 40% of the implemented reforms dealt with Action Plan priorities regarding economic and regulatory policy, trade, and the new perspective of economic cooperation with the EU' (Melnykovska & Schweickert 2008, p. 22).

This contribution is interested in understanding both external and internal drivers behind Ukraine's 'selective convergence' with EU norms. Selective convergence stands in contrast to the logic of EU Eastern Enlargement, and can be regarded as one of the most important characteristics of the implementation of the ENP. The accession states had to adopt the complete *acquis communautaire* without leaving much space for manoeuvre, but in the hope of long-term benefits from EU membership. In contrast, the neighbourhood countries do not hold short-term, or even medium-term, membership perspectives. This gives them the freedom to be much more selective in what they wish to 'pick and choose' from the EU's *acquis*. Adapting EU norms in fields like judicial reform, anti-corruption or state aid might interfere with the entrenched interests of political and economic elites.[2] Reforms in fields like social or environmental policy are not only costly but can also diminish the comparative advantages in wages and production costs that neighbourhood states hold against the EU member states. However, seemingly against all odds, empirical evidence suggests that partial convergence occurs even in policy fields that imply high costs. What explains these findings?

In order to provide an understanding of drivers and hindrances of policy change in a way that accounts for sectoral and sub-sectoral differences, this essay sketches a model that is based on empirical analysis within one policy field, environmental policy, and one country, Ukraine. Together with Georgia and Moldova, Ukraine offers one of the most likely cases of a successful adoption of EU norms due to its membership aspirations. It has often been considered as a leading example among the ENP countries and as one of the most likely to willingly import EU standards and norms. Not only does it share a border with the EU, but it also relies on the EU economically, and in terms of security policy. After the 'Orange Revolution', European integration became Ukraine's strategic priority (O'Brien 2010). A sophisticated administrative infrastructure was established to deal with legal harmonisation, including specialised institutions and departments within ministries. The Ukrainian–European Policy and Legal Advice Centre (UEPLAC) has been devoted exclusively to monitoring the process of approximation of national legislation to EU standards. While Ukraine is a country with a comparatively strong European inclination, the case of environmental policy analysed in this essay raises expectations of difficulties in norm diffusion due to the extensively high costs of convergence with EU environmental legislation (Dimitrov 2009). Observing formal adoption of EU environmental policy, as an example of policy output, the essay confirms the existence of substantial sub-sectoral differences.[3] We will argue that these differences can be explained by domestic configurations of actors and their preferences in particular policy fields. External factors, such as the EU's policy conditionality and capacity building, as well as the existence of transnational 'amplifiers' for EU norms (such as multilateral agreements or transnational networks) can also play an important role in influencing and strengthening the capacity of domestic actors favouring policy change, provided that this empowers domestic actors on the policy level to assert their goals *vis-à-vis* other sectoral interest.[4]

The time frame of the analysis is 2008–2011, but policy developments before this period are also described in order to provide some context. Operationalisation of the dependent variable is triangulated on the basis of an analysis of EU documents, reports and presentations of domestic actors, and interviews with main stakeholders. In addition, several implementation reports developed under various funding schemes by think-tank consortia dealing with monitoring the implementation of the EU–Ukraine Action Plan were used.

[2]See Ademmer and Börzel, and Langbein in this collection.
[3]For explanations of different forms of compliance, see the Introduction to this collection.
[4]See Ademmer and Börzel, and Langbein in this collection.

These were based on a common methodological framework developed by the World Wide Fund for Nature (WWF) and the Heinrich Böll Foundation, and relied on the expertise of dozens of independent policy experts over a period of several years (RAC 2009; WWF & HBS 2009; UCIPR 2010, 2011).

The remainder of the essay is structured as follows. The next section will outline the main lines of environmental policy development in Ukraine, as well as the EU's approaches to promoting environmental convergence in its neighbourhood. The following section examines the domestic veto players and the questions of the compatibility of their preferences with EU rules, and of how the EU's leverage exerted through strategies such as policy conditionality and capacity building determines policy change. The penultimate section describes patterns of policy change in four sub-fields of environmental policy. The last section summarises the empirical findings and highlights some of the conceptual problems in the EU's external governance agenda relating to convergence processes in sectoral policy fields.

Environmental policy in Ukraine and the EU as a constrained 'green normative power'

Ukraine and the EU signed a Partnership and Cooperation Agreement (PCA) in 1994, which entered into force in 1998. The document defined the goals for cooperation in 28 policy fields, environmental protection being one of these (Buzogány & Costa 2009, p. 534). Climate change and water management issues on the Danube and the Black Sea were major fields of environmental cooperation under this scheme (UNECE 2007). EU programmes in Ukraine were characterised by piecemeal technical assistance projects with limited impact due to the lack of continuity and coherent long-term sector planning (Ukraine Country Strategy Paper 2007–2013, pp. 23–25). The low importance of the environmental field was highlighted also by the modest role it played in receiving funding from the EU. Under the Eastern Partnership, framework trade, energy security and mobility issues became more pronounced. An increasing interest in legal harmonisation with EU environmental law resulted mainly from spill-over effects of Ukraine's primary goal to speed up the Free Trade Agreement with the EU. This has enforced the economic framing of environmental issues in several policy documents and coincided with the need to pass legislation related to Ukraine's World Trade Organization accession (ICPS 2007). The EU–Ukraine Action Plan outlined three main issue areas regarding environmental policy (EU–Ukraine Action Plan 2008, pp. 24–25). The first was the establishment and implementation of measures strengthening environmental governance, including the completion of administrative setup for sustainable development and the integration of environmental considerations into other policy sectors. A second goal related to 'environmental democracy', which includes strengthening environmental impact assessment (EIA) procedures and legislation on access to environmental information. The third aim was to strengthen regional and international cooperation on environmental matters, such as the need for Ukraine to implement the Kyoto Protocol as well as other multilateral environmental treaties. The environmental section of the Association Agreement underlines largely similar goals but included the need to establish a National Environmental Strategy in order to qualify for EU budget support (European Commission 2010).

Ukrainian environmental policy exhibits a combination of extensive sectoral legislation, an under-reformed system of environmental management and low levels of law enforcement

(Petkova *et al.* 2011). The structures and responsibilities for dealing with environmental policy in Ukraine have been undergoing continuous change since the breakdown of the Soviet Union (UNDP Ukraine 2007, pp. 9–11). Under these circumstances, the harmonisation of domestic legislation and administrative procedures with the blueprints provided by the EU's complex and well-developed environmental policy framework emerged as a potential opportunity for a thorough reform of Ukrainian environmental policy. While the financial and administrative capacities of the Ministry of Environment remained weak compared to the other line ministries (Petkova *et al.* 2011), some islands of excellence attracting young and well-educated professionals have developed due to the need to deal with international commitments. At the same time, the Ministry of Environment has had difficulties keeping its experienced civil servants. One of the 'survival strategies' of the Ukrainian environmental bureaucracy in order to stabilise its domestic standing was to demand binding conditions from the EU and use this as a power resource within the government.[5] Furthermore, EU environmental policy has enjoyed high levels of support in Ukraine and is regarded by 88% of opinion leaders and 68% of the public as a field where more cooperation should be promoted.[6] Working on EU-related issues has opened up new opportunities for the cash-strapped Ukrainian environmental NGOs and provided them with opportunities to become involved in externally financed project networks and tap into new funding opportunities offered by the European Commission or other donor organisations. While their influence has diminished compared to the mass mobilisations following the Chernobyl accident and the introduction of *glasnost'* (Dawson 1996, pp. 62–82; Stegny 2002; Andrusevych 2006), Ukrainian environmental civil society groups have been able to use the momentum provided by the EU's convergence agenda to demand more rights and to point to serious flaws in several fields of environmental policy making.[7]

Environmental policy is one of the most far-reaching areas of EU legislation. Nevertheless, adding an environmental dimension to the EU's relations with other states has been a protracted process which is still very much in the making and subject to numerous setbacks (del Castillo 2010). It was possible for an external 'green agenda' to gather force during the years of the EU's Eastern Enlargement, when the EU exported its whole environmental *acquis* comprising close to 200 directives into the Central and East European states. However, due to the missing conditionality element in the neighbourhood policy, expectations are tempered as to the EU's impact on neighbouring states. This can be seen in the careful wording of EU policy documents towards the neighbourhood states. Institutionally, the ENP as a policy was developed as an isomorphic replica of accession policy (Kelley 2006). In the field of environmental policy, this was reflected by the use of the term—just like in the case of former accession states—'legal approximation' in early ENP Action Plans when addressing the need for adoption of the EU *acquis* into domestic legislation. However, after some time, references to 'approximation' were replaced in the documents by the term 'convergence' which is understood to refer to a gradual and less

[5]Author's interview with a desk officer in the Directorate General for the Environment of the European Commission, 7 March 2011, Brussels.

[6]'Calm and Civilised, Like a Dog', *ENPI-INFO Series: Perceptions of the EU in Neighbourhood Partner Countries*, available at: http://www.enpi-info.eu/files/interview/a110070_ENPI_Ukraine%28EUprcptns% 29EASTen.v.3.pdf, accessed 20 September 2011.

[7]CEE Bankwatch, 'No EU Millions for Ukraine's Carbon-heavy Environment Strategy', available at: http://bankwatch.ecn.cz/project.shtml?apc = —a–1&x = 2259840, accessed 20 September 2011.

comprehensive form of alignment (European Commission 2003; Dupont & Goldenmann 2010). This change in terminology recognises the need for flexibility and the limited ability of the EU to influence change in the neighbourhood countries. EU officials have increasingly acknowledged the restricted leverage they hold over the neighbourhood countries, which is even weaker in a 'low politics' field such as the environment. The amount of direct funding that can be distributed by the EU's Directorate General for the Environment to support environmental goals is extremely limited.[8] The weakness of the EU environmental agenda in the ENP and of the environmental bureaucracy within the Commission is matched by the weakness of structures of environmental policy in Ukraine (Buzogány & Costa 2009). As a result, environmental policy conditionality remains weak and is limited to cases where Ukrainian stakeholders agree on the common ownership of these reforms or where the EU ties funding to the adoption of certain environmental policies. In practical terms, this means that the EU promotes policy change by trying to 'export' its sectoral framework directives, which are process-oriented and often merely encourage voluntary compliance processes, leaving substantial freedom in domestic implementation.

Convergence á la carte: domestic and external factors driving selective convergence

Scholarship on Europeanisation in policy studies and international relations provides a rich pool of explanatory variables accounting for policy change (Lavenex & Schimmelfennig 2009). As exemplified by research on Europeanisation in Central and Eastern European accession states, external and domestic factors are intricately interwoven. External actors may influence cost–benefit considerations, capacities or belief systems of domestic actors through a variety of different measures (Schimmelfennig & Sedelmeier 2004). Providing incentives to align with its norms and offering capacity-building measures to do so, the EU is able to empower or weaken different domestic actors active in a policy field. In this essay, we regard policy change as the result of institutional bargaining processes between Ukrainian state actors active on the levels of central government and sectoral bureaucracies, and non-state actors such as business and civil society. These actors all have different preferences and capacities concerning their countries' convergence towards EU environmental norms which are based on their expectations of being winners or losers of the adaptation process (ICPS 2007, p. 254).

Domestic veto players

Opening the 'black box' of domestic decision making allows us to differentiate between at least four groups of veto players that are particularly relevant. Institutional and partisan veto actors (Tsebelis 2002), but also informal veto players have been regarded as particularly important in the Eastern European context (see Dimitrova & Dragneva, in this collection). In Ukraine, the most important formal players are the political top-level decision makers, such as the Cabinet of Ministers and the Presidential Administration. However, the division of power is far from clear. According to the Bertelsmann Transformation Index, within the Ukrainian government

---

[8]Author's interview with desk officer in the Directorate General for the Environment of the European Commission, 7 March 2011, Brussels.

competing interests are partially reflected in institutional duplication, such as the existence of several administrative units with similar (formal) tasks that compete for decision-making power and which can be seen in the rivalry that exists between the presidential administration and individual ministries. The undefined relations between the institutions of the presidency, government and parliament continue to cause friction and contribute to the political crisis, which is exacerbated by personal interests of top government officials. The veto powers repeatedly try to instrumentalise the formal system and undermine it without questioning the system as such. (Bertelsmann Stiftung 2009, p. 8)

Moreover, government bodies aggregating various political, regional, economic and sectoral interests are often described as being open to specific 'oligarchic' forms of interference (Wilson 2005). At the same time, staff within line ministries vary in their orientation and sympathy towards the East (Russia) or the West (Europe) due to different path dependencies in their recruiting policies (Biberman 2011). Our focus on 'low politics' reminds us of the importance of sectoral administration within the Ministry of Environment and Natural Resources and its specialised sub-units, staffed by policy experts in charge of the day-by-day handling of policy issues, including questions of convergence with EU norms. As noted in the previous section, the Ukrainian environmental branch can be regarded as weak. Sectoral bureaucracy is often torn between two contrasting adaptation strategies concerning EU policies. On the one hand, it can support convergence with EU rules for professional and bureaucratic reasons: the EU can help by introducing comprehensive blueprints that are, in most of the cases, of superior quality to domestic legislation. At the same time, the EU's influence also enables weak bureaucracies to act strategically and strengthen their standing *vis-à-vis* other domestic actors (Buzogány & Costa 2009). On the other hand, EU rules can also trigger a shift in regulatory power from public regulation, which is firmly embedded in the mindsets of regulators in the post-Soviet area (Ehrke 2010; Langbein 2010b), to greater openness towards non-state actors, which might, in turn, be associated with weakening the sectoral public administration.

Indeed, in addition to state actors, non-state actors, in both business and civil society, are actively involved in supporting or opposing alignment with external rules as this might provide them with economic benefits or influence over policy outputs (Melnykovska & Schweickert 2008). Strengthening the influence of environmental NGOs was an important policy tool used by the Commission to reinforce the adoption of the *acquis* in the accession states (Börzel & Buzogány 2010), and it can be seen at work also in the case of countries such as Ukraine (Stewart 2009; Wetzel 2010). While environmental NGOs in Ukraine will rarely hold veto powers, big business certainly does to such an extent that, in certain cases, it can be considered to be 'state capture'. However, in terms of political and economic preferences, influential business actors in Ukraine are far from being monolithic. While some might fear that growing alignment with the EU will affect them negatively, other branches can be regarded as 'bottom-up' forces of Europeanisation (Melnykovska & Schweickert 2008). Indeed, as Ukraine shares intensive economic ties with the EU, the planned adoption of the Deep and Comprehensive Free Trade Agreement (DCFTA) generates considerable profit opportunities for business elites interested in exporting to EU markets (Langbein 2010a). Incentives for convergence with EU norms include not only access to EU markets but also raising attractiveness for foreign investments in the Ukraine. Adding to this, Ukrainian business actors can hope that convergence with EU norms can raise the credibility and certainty of domestic reforms due to improved governance structures. Depending on export structure and the expected benefits from access to EU markets, increased regulatory harmonisation can become an important trigger for business actors to embrace convergence with EU norms (Melnykovska & Schweickert 2008). On the other hand, the costs of non-convergence with EU norms can also be high as EU market access can be restricted for products not complying with EU standards. Thus, both multinational and domestic companies may be interested in promoting the adoption of technically up-to-date standards and regulatory procedures in order to increase their presence and competiveness on the Ukrainian market (Vogel & Kagan 2004).

Preferential fit, policy conditionality and capacity building

Based on the literature on Europeanisation and external governance, this essay argues that policy change in Ukrainian environmental policy is a function of preferential fit between EU incentives and preferences of domestic veto players; EU policy conditionality reducing the costs of change for veto players; and targeted capacity-building efforts towards key actors in a given policy sub-field. We expect that policy change towards EU norms is more likely if the preferences of sectoral veto players and EU incentives are compatible. Due to the high costs of convergence, the willingness of key veto players to implement policy change depends essentially on the 'preferential fit' between the EU's sectoral policies and the preferences of veto players (Ademmer & Börzel, in this collection). If there is no 'preferential fit', the EU has two strategies to mitigate the veto player's high costs raised by adaptation to its norms: policy conditionality and capacity building.

The EU's policy conditionality works through rewards and sanctions that empower some players to the detriment of others. Scholarship on 'Europeanisation' in Central and Eastern Europe underlines the importance of the 'external incentives model' behind the success of EU conditionality (Schimmelfennig & Sedelmeier 2004, p. 664). While the conditionality exerted under the ENP is much weaker in offering incentives for convergence, the 'external incentives model' can still explain the different speed and depth of convergence processes on the policy level (Gawrich *et al.* 2010, p. 1216). To be sure, the lack of a clear membership perspective in the ENP undermines all attempts to promote policy convergence by 'hierarchy' (Knill & Tosun 2009). However, the EU has attempted to solve this structural problem both through 'sequencing' incentives (Wolczuk 2010, pp. 50–52) and remaining rhetorically ambiguous about the long-term accession perspectives of the neighbourhood countries (Youngs 2009). While this is a much weaker instrument than the EU's membership conditionality used during the accession period of the Central and Eastern European countries, it can still be influential on the sectoral preferences of governments. This can happen if policy change is tied to specific rewards, such as funding opportunities, access to EU markets, possibilities of technological modernisation or gains in legitimacy, which reduce the costs of adaptation for some veto players (Ademmer & Börzel, in this collection).

However, the neighbourhood countries often simply lack the capacity needed for policy change. Therefore, the EU, often in concert with other like-minded donors, uses the second strategy of external capacity building in order to strengthen capacity of both state and non-state actors (Bruszt & McDermott 2009). In doing so, it has largely replicated the policy instruments from its accession policy and provides financial resources (such as budget

TABLE 1
FACTORS DRIVING THE SELECTIVE ADOPTION OF EU ENVIRONMENTAL NORMS IN UKRAINE

	Preferential fit	Conditionality	Capacity	Outcome
Climate change	+	−	−	Adoption/emerging behavioural compliance
Environmental governance	−	+	−	Adoption/lack of behavioural compliance
Water management	−	−	+	Selective adoption, emerging behavioural compliance
Environmental democracy	−	−	−	Inertia

support) or technical assistance or expertise also under the ENP. Ideally, such assistance programmes can strengthen state capacity by addressing the capability of public officials to design policies (Peters 2005). Strengthening policy capacity can take place through many different channels but previous experience shows that the way in which external assistance is distributed, the type of assistance and the level at which it is applied have a strong influence on outcomes (Sedelmeier 2008; Langbein 2010b). Adding to its own direct external assistance, the European Commission often resorts also to norms adopted in multilateral treaties or uses transnational networks in order to strengthen its leverage externally (Freyburg *et al.* 2009, p. 918). Working in concert with other like-minded international institutions can increase available funding and make use of scale and synergy effects. Besides relying on international treaties and organisations, the EU often uses transnational networks to strengthen the efficiency and legitimacy of its external rule promotion (Lavenex & Schimmelfennig 2009). Horizontal expert networks formed by regulators, business actors and NGOs also play an important role in promoting functional integration between the EU and its neighbours. Functional spill-over of EU policies into the neighbouring countries, ranging from migration and internal security (Lavenex & Wichmann 2009) to energy (Hofer 2008) and environment (Stulberg & Lavenex 2007; Buzogány & Costa 2009), has created the need for regulatory coordination. Even if the effectiveness of such networks often suffers from cultural and technical differences or from the lack of political support (Wolczuk 2009), they can provide EU officials with means of controlling the domestic implementation of European requirements.

Selective convergence of Ukrainian environmental policies with EU norms

This section presents four case studies illustrating how preferential fit, policy conditionality and capacity building interact in producing policy change (see Table 1). In the case of climate change policy, the EU's expectations rely on the Kyoto Protocol, which is highly beneficial to Ukraine. Policy change here was internally driven, as major Ukrainian industrial conglomerates were interested in becoming active on the global greenhouse gas (GHG) market. Thus, Ukrainian rule adoption and emerging behavioural compliance was prompted by the preferential fit between EU rules and the preferences of these actors. The cases of environmental governance and water management show that where EU rules do not fit preferences of powerful domestic actors, capacity building or policy-specific conditionality is needed to mitigate the high costs for these powerful actors. The case of environmental governance illustrates that if preferential misfit is mitigated by policy-specific conditionality, the likelihood of rule adoption increases. In this case, the EU has tied its budget support to the development of framework documents that outline the medium-term policy perspective in the environmental sector. Besides offering financial rewards for doing so, the EU has also provided support for 'bottom-up' pressure coming from environmental NGOs. As a result, opposition to formulating these documents was reduced and the Ukrainian government adopted the National Environmental Policy Strategy. However, as the rewards were only tied to adoption of this document, behavioural compliance was lacking.

The case of water management shows that if 'preferential misfit' is mitigated by external capacity building, the likelihood of rule adoption may increase, even if in a selective and incremental way. While the water management sector had been subject to substantial international capacity-building efforts since the late 2000s, these remained largely disjointed and a thorough reform process was impeded by other sectors with a stronger leverage on the executive. Finally, the case of environmental democracy is used to show that if preferential misfit is not mitigated by policy-specific conditionality or by external capacity building, the likelihood of inertia is high. In the case of legislation relating to environmental democracy, domestic supporters remained largely insulated by more powerful veto players whose preferences were adversely affected by these new rules and both comprehensive policy conditionality and external capacity building arrived too late.

Climate change: adoption and emerging behavioural compliance

In the case of climate change policy, Ukrainian rule adoption and its emerging behavioural compliance were supported by the 'preferential fit' between the EU's expectations and preferences of key domestic actors. Influential Ukrainian business actors from the energy sector and heavy industries were interested in becoming active in the GHG market. Policy change occurred here even without explicit EU policy conditionality or capacity building as the market access for Ukrainian companies provided them with sufficient incentives. The EU–Ukraine Association Agenda mentioned among its main goals the 'implementation of the Kyoto Protocol through a dialogue within the Joint EU–Ukraine Working Group on Climate Change on a new post-2012 agreement on climate change, on eligibility criteria for using the Kyoto mechanisms, and on developing measures to mitigate and adapt to climate change' (European Commission 2010, p. 11). Due to its inefficient heavy industries and the energy losses in its heating sector, Ukraine is among the highest GHG emitters worldwide.[9] Nevertheless, the industrial decline that occurred after the collapse of the Soviet Union allows Ukraine to increase its GHG emission levels as these are at merely two-thirds of where they were in 1990. In fact, the emission trading system under the Kyoto Protocol makes Ukraine one of the most important players on the global GHG market. Business actors, both domestic and multinational, have been influential in installing an institutional framework that serves their needs (BFAI 2007). For business actors, the Kyoto Protocol provided incentives to develop joint implementation (JI) projects in order to trade with carbon credits and secure funding and expertise for technological modernisation from

---

[9]The ratio (index) of CO_2 emissions per GDP unit for Ukraine is 7,483 metric tons of CO_2 per \$1 million of GDP, *vis-à-vis* the world average of 846 and the European average of 640.

Western multinationals. In order to benefit from mechanisms of the Kyoto Treaty, Ukraine adopted a legislative framework, created an inventory system of GHG emission and adopted a new institutional infrastructure. Secondary legislation was adopted in order to clear the way for emissions trade and JI projects (Borysova 2010). In March 2008, the responsibility for JI was attributed to a new government body, the National Environmental Investment Agency (NEIA).[10] Clearly, the steps taken focused on the flexible mechanisms of the Kyoto Protocol, which Ukraine was able to fulfil easily and thus gain financial benefits (Korppoo & Moe 2008). According to the EU's Progress Reports, some 81 projects were under development in 2009, with more proposals being approved. In 2009, the state budget received €320 million to finance green investments from selling its national GHG quota to Japan. Among the main domestic drivers of JI development were national business conglomerates, represented by the Ukrainian Union of Industrialists and Global Compact Ukraine, many of whose members were closely linked to heavy industry in Eastern Ukraine and, as such, they were potential JI developers.[11] System Management Consulting (SCM), the business conglomerate of one of the country's main 'oligarchs', Rinat Akhmetov, has become a key player in the 'hot air' business as its power and steel plants are major emitters and therefore a priority for investment (Mendoza-Wilson & Skarshevskiy 2011). The extent of SCM's influence over Ukrainian climate policy is highlighted by the fact that SCM's representatives took part in UN climate negotiations as a part of the Ukrainian official delegation.[12]

In sum, the EU has relied on mechanisms of the Kyoto Protocol and on market forces rather than policy conditionality and capacity building to induce climate change policies in Ukraine. As the construction of the Kyoto Protocol is beneficial to Ukraine, this allows domestic business actors to sell their 'historical' surplus carbon credits on the global market. Directly benefiting from the flexible mechanisms, domestic industry has become a driver implementing those provisions of the Kyoto Protocol where it could gain profits. However, all attempts to reduce GHG emissions or to introduce binding environmental standards that go beyond the Kyoto goals are cautiously blocked by business actors (UCIPR 2011, p. 64). While policy change is indeed taking place in this case, its effects are contradictory. Ukrainian environmental organisations have repeatedly pointed to the 'double standards' of the Kyoto system, which allows companies to reap benefits without having to comply with a transparent 'green investment' scheme (Stavcuk 2008). The environmental NGO Environment–People–Law (EPL) has initiated litigation in order to uncover the opaque usage of funds received through JI projects. According to Ukrainian legislation, funds received through the GHG trading system must be spent on environmental projects. However, such deals were typically kept confidential. Using access to environmental information legislation, EPL requested the National Environmental Investment Agency and the Ministry of Environmental details about the Ukrainian funds received by selling carbon credits (Kravchenko 2010). After his election as the President of Ukraine, Victor Yanukovych announced that $375 million which were received through GHG trade under the Kyoto Protocol had been 'plundered' by the former

---

[10]It was renamed the State Agency of Environmental Investments in 2010.

[11]Global Compact Ukraine, *Third Ukrainian Business Summit on Climate Change: Energy in Focus*, available at: http://www.globalcompact.org.ua/press/news/431, accessed 20 September 2011. 'The State Environmental Investment Agency Signed a Cooperation Agreement with the Ukrainian Union of Industrialists and Entrepreneurs', available at: http://www.neia.gov.ua/nature/control/en/publish/article; jsessionid = EB0F50A48699E5BA3F8B0285B5A4A4AE?art_id = 124901&cat_id = 42452, accessed 20 September 2011.

[12]Author's interview (via e-mail), Ukrainian environmental NGO, 22 March 2011.

Tymoshenko government. The former government was accused with violating the terms of the Kyoto Protocol by misappropriating these funds to shore up the finances of the country's pension fund and to purchase ambulances.[13] Based on this and several other charges, Tymoshenko was sentenced to seven years in prison.[14]

Environmental governance: adoption without behavioural compliance

A key environmental commitment made by Ukraine under the Association Agenda concerned the 'development, adoption and implementation of a National Environmental Policy Strategy and of a National Action Plan 2009–2012 that implements this until the end of the year 2010' (European Commission 2010, p. 9). According to the EU, these policy documents should lead the reform process and have been identified as the major condition for Ukraine to receive sectoral budget support from the EU amounting to €25 million, with an additional top-up option worth €10 million from the Swedish government. The Strategy had to include concrete steps in institutional capacity building, legislative measures dealing with convergence to sectoral EU principles, and the execution of international conventions and multilateral agreements on environmental protection. Adopting the Strategy was mentioned as the only environmental policy issue on the list of urgent reforms in the 'Füle Matrix',[15] the EU thus signalling clearly that it was 'serious' about this document.

The adoption of far-reaching environmental goals was seen as particularly problematic by the energy and industry branches within the state administration, such as the Ministry of Infrastructure, the Ministry of Energy and Coal Industry, and the Ministry of Construction, Housing and Utilities, which were essentially captured by oligarchic interest groups (Avioutskii 2010). Ukraine started working on the Concept of the National Environmental Policy and the Draft of the National Environmental Strategy in 2007, planning to adopt it in 2009. The initial draft was prepared by UEPLAC after consultations with environmental organisations, experts and parliamentarians of the *Verkhovna Rada*. After changes in the government, UEPLAC's draft was dismissed as being too process-oriented but central government authorities delayed preparing a new one.

When the deadline to meet the EU's expectations became pressing, the Ministry of Environment reached out for support from the European Commission as well as from Germany and Sweden to draft a new document. Civil society organisations holding technical and legal expertise in environmental policy matters, such as the non-governmental organisations MAMA-86, the National Ecological Centre of Ukraine and the Ukrainian Ecological League, sought to participate in the drafting process, but were informed about the contents of the Strategy only two weeks after the draft strategy had been referred to the *Verkhovna Rada*.[16] Due to criticism from environmental civil society groups, the Ministry of Environmental Protection had to reschedule the hearing so that NGOs could provide their

---

[13]'Tymoshenko Charged with Misspending', *Financial Times*, 20 December 2010.

[14]'Yulia Tymoshenko Sentenced to Seven Years in Prison', *The Guardian*, 11 October 2011.

[15]The 'Füle Matrix' is a document presented by the EU Commissioner Štefan Füle in Kyiv on 22 April 2010. The plan previews implementation of concrete measures, aimed at attracting macro-financial assistance from the EU, improving access for Ukrainian goods to the European markets and reforming the technical regulation system.

[16]'Letter from Iryna Holovko to José Manuel Pinto Teixeira, Head of European Commission Delegation in Ukraine', *CEE Bankwatch*, available at: http://www.necu.org.ua/wp-content/uploads/bwn_letter_ukraine_bs_10-10.pdf, accessed 20 September 2011.

comments. Nevertheless, the draft document was passed to parliament without any changes only one day later. In an open letter addressed to the European Commission, environmental organisations the National Ecological Center of Ukraine and MAMA-86, together with the Prague-based umbrella group the Central and Eastern European Bankwatch Network, voiced concern that the drafting of the Strategy, a main condition for receiving EU funds, took place without effective public participation, thus contradicting both Ukrainian and European legislation. In response, the Commission made clear to the Ukrainian government that no EU funds could be transferred to Ukraine unless the government became more open to input from civil society.[17]

The threat of losing budget support alerted the central governmental authorities and silenced opposition within government. Furthermore, potential veto players were taken by surprise by the fast-track approach suddenly emphasised by the government.[18] At the second hearing of the drafts the dialogue between the public and ministry representatives was productive and most NGO comments concerning technical details and participatory rights were included into the draft (UCIPR 2011, p. 17).

Thus, by the end of the year, Ukraine was able to finalise the preparation of the draft documents needed for a financing agreement on budgetary support to Ukraine's environmental sector.[19] The successful adoption of the National Environmental Policy Strategy and the National Action Plan implementing it shows that the clear conditionality of the EU was influential, not only in moving Ukraine towards policy change, but also in providing domestic environmental civil society organisations an opportunity to press for their inclusion. Thus, the EU's policy conditionality was useful for at least temporarily overriding domestic veto players, leading to partial policy change in the formal adoption of the National Environmental Strategy. Nevertheless, this was not coupled with behavioural change, which makes the sustainability of the adopted policies questionable. Indeed, after the Ukrainian government received sectoral budget support, the environmental NGO MAMA-86 reported that the Secretariat of the Cabinet of Ministers had begun rewriting the National Environmental Plan, deleting several of its core provisions previously agreed with the EU.[20]

Water management: selective rule adoption, emerging behavioural compliance

The annexes of the EU–Ukraine Association Agenda also mention compliance with multilateral environmental conventions regarding water management, such as the (Helsinki) Convention on the Protection and Use of Transboundary Watercourses and International Lakes and the (Bucharest) Convention on the Protection of the Black Sea Against Pollution, as goals that Ukraine needs to make progress on. In addition, Ukraine voluntarily committed itself to comply with the principles of the EU's Water Framework Directive (WFD, 2000/60/European Communities) (European Communities 2000). In the case of water

[17]'Ukraine's Environment Strategy Worrying Brussels', *EUobserver*, available at: http://euobserver.com/9/30887, accessed 20 September 2011.

[18]Author's interview (by e-mail), Ukrainian environmental NGO, 12 March 2011.

[19]*Zakon Ukrainy*, No. 2818, adopted 21 December 2010.

[20]'The Secretariat of Cabinet Ministers of Ukraine Rewrote the National Environmental Plan', MAMA-86, available at: http://www.mama-86.org.ua/index.php/en/ecologization/ecointegration-news/263-neap.html, accessed 20 September 2011.

management policy, adopting EU water management norms in Ukraine implies a departure from the Soviet-style resource management approach which emphasised water use and infrastructure construction rather than resource conservation and protection. While the MENR and its local structures are in charge of environmental monitoring of water issues, the most influential player in the water sector is the State Committee for Water Management (*Vodhosp*),[21] which has command over important personal and infrastructural resources at national and local levels. As a result of long-term external capacity building, *Vodhosp* supports the (selective) introduction of EU water management principles, such as the establishment of integrated river basin management. However, rule adoption remains highly selective, as the long-term costs of the envisioned changes are not mitigated by external support and important veto players associated with the State Committee on Housing and Municipal Economy (*Derzhzhytlokomunhosp*), now the Ministry of Municipal Housing Economy and the regions (*oblasti*), remain influential in blocking policy change.

Ukraine based the reform of its water management institution on principles of integrated water management in the late 1990s. The *Verkhovna Rada* adopted the Water Code of Ukraine in 2002, introducing the principle of river basin-based management, which is a central aspect of the WFD. However, it failed to spell out how this should be implemented. Institutional changes included the establishment of nine main river basin management structures (*baseinovoe upravlenye vodnych resursov*, BUVR) as part of *Vodhosp*. In addition, water councils were set up on several river basins, even if they lacked power and a solid legal basis. For the Ukrainian water management administration, the WFD served as a welcome example to give a new momentum to the stalled domestic reform process. International organisations such as the United Nations Development Programme (UNDP), the World Bank and the bilateral and multilateral donor community have been active in advising water management reforms in Ukraine from the 1990s onwards. In 2002, the Organisation for Security and Cooperation in Europe (OSCE) organised seminars for Ukrainian water management stakeholders and promoted the introduction of norms highlighted by the EU's WFD.[22] From the second half of the 2000s, EU capacity building became the most important trigger for domestic policy change. Beginning in 2007, two large, multi-year projects, funded by the European Commission under programmes such as Technical Assistance to the Commonwealth of Independent States (TACIS) and EuropeAid, strengthened the capacity of Ukrainian water management bodies.[23] Both provided help in preparing changes to the Water Code and to secondary laws and regulations based on EU water legislation and the principles of Integrated Water Resource Management.[24] Parallel to the capacity building in these projects, Ukrainian water management experts actively participated in various common networks bringing together experts both from the region and the EU member states, such as the EU Water Initiative, the International Commission for the Protection of the Danube River or the Commission on the Protection of the Black Sea against Pollution. Particularly important were experiences won in developing Integrated

[21]It was renamed the State Agency of Water Resources (*Derzhvodahentstvo*) in 2010.

[22]'OSCE Holds Second Roundtable on Water Management in Ukraine', available at: http://www.osce.org/ukraine/54862, accessed 20 September 2011.

[23]See http://www.ecbsea.org and http://www.wgw.org.ua, last accessed 19 April 2011.

[24]Mott MacDonald, 'Water Governance in the Western EECCA Countries', Tacis/2008/137–153 (EC) Project Completion Report, available at: http://www.wgw.org.ua/publications/Water%20Governance_Project%20Completion%20Report_Final.pdf, accessed 20 September 2011.

River Basin Management Plans for trans-boundary areas of water, such as the Tisa River, where Ukrainian experts worked closely with their colleagues from the new EU member states to implement the provisions of the WFD. Driven by neighbouring states, external donors and enthusiastic experts within the water management administration, the draft National Program for Water Management Development put forward a unified strategy for developing Ukraine's water management system, meeting some new methodological requirements along with the objectives of the WFD (European Commission 2011, p. 18).

However, policy change on the domestic level has only taken place incrementally. As water management is a cross-cutting issue involving many policy areas and actors, the importance of political support for such policy changes at the level of central government is crucial. However, the opposing interests of water management actors and other intersecting policy fields, such as housing and industry, have prevented redrafting the Water Code of 2002 which is now regarded as largely obsolete. As a result, policy changes in the water management sector are usually regulated through lower level ministerial ordinances (*nakazy*), which do not carry the weight of a law or a governmental decree (*postanova*). The EU's capacity building focused on legal harmonisation plans and strategies within the water management sector. Implementing the envisioned changes has given rise to excessively high costs that are not met through external assistance. As a result, while consensus exists within the water management community about the aim of full harmonisation with EU water management objectives, at the political level the government has regularly shied away from extensive policy changes. One particular reason for this incrementalism is institutional: Ukrainian water management suffers from unclear and overlapping competencies of the different bodies in charge of water quality and quantity issues. While the Ministry of the Environment and National Resources has been in charge of water management, drinking-water provision is regulated by the much stronger Ministry of Housing and Communal Services. At the same time, there is also interference from the State Committee for Water Management (*Vodhosp*) and the regions (*oblasti*), with both regarding water management issues as their responsibility. In addition, administrative reforms introduced by the Yanukovich government in 2010 'practically annulled the [Environmental] Ministry's ability to achieve results in this field' (UCIPR 2011, p. 67), as the institutions selected to implement integrated water resources management had lost their competences.

Despite numerous hindrances however, there have been some signs of a strengthening of reform-minded constituencies within the state water management sector and among non-state actors which, in the medium term, may help promote reforms. Western water companies and technology providers have started looking towards the Ukrainian water market, which is in need of expertise and investment.[25] Convergence towards EU norms could secure a large market once the modernisation of this sector in Ukraine is decided upon. Business actors here share common interests with environmental NGOs. Supported by the Ukraine Water Partnership, a quasi-NGO that is part of the Global Water Partnership network and which represents important stakeholders from the global water industry, the Ukrainian environmental NGO MAMA-86 came forward with an assessment of the draft National Program for Water Management, which included constructive proposals for its upgrading (GWP 2010). However, while external capacity building has helped disseminate

[25]German Water Partnership, Regional Section Ukraine, available at: http://www.germanwaterpartnership. de/index.php?option = com_content&view = article&id = 461&Itemid = 226&lang = en, accessed 20 September 2011.

the principles of the EU water policy through various transnational networks and international institutions acting in concert, overall policy change in the Ukrainian water management sector has remained rather disappointing. This can be explained by the high costs of these reforms for actors outside the water management sector as well as the lack of policy-specific conditionality. Nevertheless, in the medium term, the potential for externally triggered change may increase if non-state actors start to put pressure on the government to adopt policy change.

Environmental democracy: inertia

In the case of policies regarding 'environmental democracy', the preferences of key veto players interested in construction and industrial development have opposed any policy change that could endanger their activities. So far, the limited policy conditionality and the late capacity building by the EU for actors in support of policy change, such as the MENR and environmental civil society groups, has not been able to provide sufficient support for changing the *status quo*. Enhancing the quality of 'environmental democracy' also figures prominently among the main goals agreed between the EU and the Ukrainian government. In practical terms, 'environmental democracy' covers legislation offering participatory rights to stakeholders. On the international level, such legislation is mainly condensed in the Aarhus and Espoo Convention. The rather loosely formulated expectation of Ukraine is mentioned twice in the EU document: the EU expects further development and implementation of Ukrainian environmental legislation, strategies and plans, in particular on environmental impact assessment, strategic environmental assessment, access to environmental information and public participation, and refers also to 'further development of national implementation instruments in line with multilateral environmental agreements'(European Commission 2010, pp. 7–8).

While basic legislation and key procedures for environmental impact assessment (EIA) have been in place in Ukraine since the early 1990s, when the country became the first Soviet republic to pass regulations on access to environmental information and EIA (*ekologichna expertiza*) (Zaharchenko 2010), these laws differed substantially from EU standards.[26] Despite the EU's ongoing obsession with these core instruments of environmental planning, its success in moving Ukraine towards upgrading its legislation has been limited so far and Ukraine has repeatedly failed to adopt the provisions of the Espoo and the Aarhus Conventions. While the country established an 'Aarhus Information and Training Center' and adopted Action Plans addressing its compliance with the Convention, the Environmental Ministry was unable to override opposition by more powerful domestic veto players representing sectoral interest groups (RAC 2009). While the MENR established an inter-ministerial working group on these issues, more powerful ministries such as the Ministry of Infrastructure and the Ministry for Regional Development, Building and Housing, which are well-connected with the 'construction lobby', hindered the implementation of any meaningful reform.[27] Indeed, while the Ministry of Environment and Natural Resources and the NGO community supported full convergence with the EU's EIA

[26]Author's interview with desk officer in the Directorate General for the Environment of the European Commission, 7 March 2011, Brussels.

[27]Author's interview (via e-mail), Ukrainian environmental NGO, 28 September 2011.

Directive (European Communities 2001), after external attention to Ukraine's convergence in environmental policy had diminished due to the adoption of the National Environmental Policy Strategy in 2010, the government even hollowed out the existing EIA by adopting a new law on urban planning[28] which practically annuls the EIA (Andrusevych 2011; RAC 2011; UCIPR 2011, p. 21). As a result, the Aarhus Convention's Compliance Committee underlined that Ukraine was still not in compliance and threatened sanctions on Ukraine, including exclusion from the Convention, if it failed to comply by the time of the Fourth Meeting of Parties in 2011.[29]

Nevertheless, the fact that the EU has thrown its weight behind the Aarhus Convention still strengthens domestic environmental actors to some extent. The NGO EPL filed cases against the government of Ukraine challenging the government's decision to dig a deep-water navigation channel through Ukraine's portion of the Danube Delta Reserve (Wetzel 2010). The court based EPL's *locus standi* on the Aarhus Convention, which Ukraine had ratified, even though it had not adopted any implementing legislation.

While the EU had limited means to provide strong incentives for domestic veto players to comply with provisions of the Conventions, it was also quite late in engaging in capacity building for the environmental bureaucracy. By the end of 2009, the Commission launched two projects carried out by German and Danish consulting companies, which assisted Ukrainian environmental authorities to fulfil their commitments under the Aarhus and Espoo Conventions.[30] As a result, a draft decree was promulgated incorporating the approach used in EU legislation and the Espoo Convention, including its protocols on Strategic Environmental Assessment. In addition, a draft regulation about the participation of civil society in environmental decision making was prepared which responded to complaints Ukraine received for not fulfilling its duties under the Aarhus convention (UCIPR 2011). However, whether these drafts will indeed be used by the Ukrainian government is rather unlikely as policy change is blocked by strong domestic veto players, while external capacity building is limited and policy conditionality absent.

Conclusion

Reforms of the environmental legislative framework in Ukraine, if they occurred, have been based largely on concepts of relevant European legislation. However, policy change has taken place selectively. This essay has highlighted the importance of domestic veto players for policy change and argued that the differences can be explained by the 'preferential fit' between EU incentives and preferences of domestic veto players, as well as the influence of EU policy conditionality and capacity building.

The case studies illustrated that selective rule adoption and behavioural compliance can occur even in a country that lacks membership aspirations, depending on the domestic configuration of actors and their preferences in particular policy fields. Where EU rules fit the

[28]*Zakon Ukrainy*, No. 3038 of 17 February 2011, available at: http://zakon2.rada.gov.ua/laws/show/3038-17, accessed 15 November 2012.

[29]'Outcomes of the 4th Meeting of Parties to the Aarhus Convention', Resource and Analysis Center 'Society and Environment', available at: http://www.rac.org.ua/fileadmin/user_upload/documents/weekly_reviews/ENG/05_07_2011_Aarhus_MOP4_ENG.pdf, accessed 20 September 2011.

[30]'EU Support to Ukraine to Implement the ESPOO and AARHUS Conventions', 30 July 2010, available at: http://eeas.europa.eu/delegations/ukraine/press_corner/all_news/news/2010/20100730_1_en.htm, accessed 20 September 2011.

preferences of powerful veto players, rule adoption and emerging behavioural compliance occurs in the absence of conditionality and capacity building. The case of climate change policy highlighted the possibility of policy change happening despite high costs, weak policy conditionality and weak external capacity building, if powerful veto players' preferences fit EU policies. If EU rules do not fit the preferences of powerful domestic veto players, policy-specific conditionality or capacity building can mitigate high adaptational costs (Ademmer & Börzel, in this collection). The case of the adaptation of the EU's prescription relating to environmental governance in Ukraine shows that 'reinforcement by reward' (Schimmelfennig & Sedelmeier 2004) works also in the context of a neighbourhood country, even if only smaller 'carrots' than membership, such as budget support, are offered. In this case, veto players did not interfere and domestic pro-convergence actors were empowered by EU policy conditionality. However, as the rewards were only tied to the adoption of a policy framework document and the EU's policy conditionality could not trigger behavioural compliance, this case also hints at the difficulties of maintaining a reform momentum when the rewards have already been reaped.[31] The case of water management showed that substantial external capacity building has indeed led to some reforms, but these remain limited and often contradictory. Reform plans often remain with the environmental administration, which lacks the political influence to push through its sectoral interests against more powerful veto players. Capacity problems of the sectoral environmental administration, its weak standing within the government, its lack of financial resources to implement reform projects all remained prevalent and could not be mitigated by the financially limited support of external actors. These influences were too weak, too uncoordinated or addressed merely technical issues without taking into account the political process. Finally, the case of environmental democracy illustrated that if the incompatibility of EU expectations and preferences of domestic veto players is not addressed by policy-specific conditionality or by external capacity building, the likelihood of inertia (either by formal adoption or behavioural compliance) remains high.

These findings about the success and failure of the policy change in Ukrainian environmental policy show the benefits, but also the potential pitfalls, of a sectoral policy-oriented approach to the study of the EU's neighbourhood policy. In this context, we need to keep in mind the case-specific constellations, which contrast Ukraine with some of the other countries in the region. Indeed, Ukraine has often been considered to be one of the most willing pro-European reformers. Its European inclination is partially supported by geographic and cultural proximity, business orientation and public opinion. At the same time, its geopolitical importance and the sheer size of its internal market also make the Ukraine an important potential partner for the EU. This contextual factor might be less supportive in the case of other neighbourhood countries. However, this essay suggests that the sub-sectoral variations of convergence found in Ukraine imply a rather limited transferability of the causal mechanisms driving convergence from one country or policy field to the next. Thus, both policy practitioners and researchers are well-advised to refrain from 'one size fits all' explanations when they design policies for the neighbourhood countries or try to understand similar developments.

Studies of convergence with EU rules in the neighbourhood countries often assume that 'institutional density' drives policy change, and that policy fields that are more institutionalised (internationally) are more likely to converge towards EU norms. Based

---

[31]For a discussion of this problem in the context of Central and East European states, see Dimitrova (2010).

on the certainly limited empirical evidence in the four cases discussed here, this assumption receives only partial support. While climate change, water management and environmental governance can all be considered to be highly institutionalised, on the domestic level only climate change policy witnessed clear policy change as a result of supportive domestic veto players. This example illustrates again that domestic contextual factors have to be taken into consideration more explicitly.

The essay also suggests that 'low politics' fields, which are often credited with being potentially promising sectors of trans-boundary collaboration and convergence, have to be treated in a differentiated manner. As we find variance even within different 'low politics' fields, explanations focusing on policy type alone seem to have their limits when explaining policy change. Again, factors leading and hindering convergence need to be qualified. Rather than institutional density or policy type as explanations for policy change, the essay underlines the role of domestic preferences and capacities which can be influenced by external factors. The essay shows that particularly non-state actors, both in business and civil society can play a role in leading convergence—but only if convergence with EU norms provides them with profits or influence. Whether these drivers will have an impact or not remains a matter of 'high politics'. Not only does the EU need to agree internally about the benefits it wants to share and to reach a common understanding of the *finalité* of the convergence process (Wolczuk 2010, p. 46), but also the neighbourhood countries have to make firm and binding decisions about which part of the *á la carte* menu offered by the EU they want to order.

German Public Administration Research Institute

References

Albi, A. (2009) 'The EU's "External Governance" and Legislative Approximation by Neighbours: Challenges for the Classic Constitutional Templates', *European Foreign Affairs Review*, 14, 2.

Andrusevych, A. (2006) 'Neuriadovi ekologichni organizatsii v Ukrainii: problemi stanovlenia ta razvitku', *JI*, 41, 4.

Andrusevych, A. (2011) 'Aarhus Rake. Attempt No 3', *Environmental Policy and Law Weekly*, 14–18 March

Avioutskii, V. (2010) 'The Consolidation of Ukrainian Business Clans', *Revue internationale d'intelligence économique*, 2, 1.

Barbé, E., Costa, O., Herranz Surrallés, A. & Natorski, M. (2009) 'Which Rules Shape EU External Governance? Patterns of Rule Selection in Foreign and Security Policies', *Journal of European Public Policy*, 16, 6.

Barbé, E. & Johansson-Nogués, E. (2008) 'The EU as a Modest "Force for Good": The European Neighbourhood Policy', *International Affairs*, 84, 1.

Bertelsmann Stiftung (2009) *BTI 2010—Ukraine Country Report* (Gütersloh, Bertelsmann Stiftung).

BFAI (2007) *JI-Market Brief Ukraine* (Cologne, Bundesagentur für Aussenwirtschaft).

Biberman, Y. (2011) 'Bureaucratic Partisanship and State Building', *Problems of Post-Communism*, 58, 2.

Borysova, I. (2010) 'Ukraine zwischen Kopenhagen und Mexiko', *ukraine analysen*, 73/10.

Börzel, T. (2010) *The Transformative Power of Europe Reloaded: The Limits of External Europeanization* KFG Working Paper Series, No. 11 (Berlin, Freie Universität Berlin).

Börzel, T. & Buzogány, A. (2010) 'Environmental Organisations and the Europeanisation of Public Policy in Central and Eastern Europe: The Case of Biodiversity Governance', *Environmental Politics*, 19, 5.

Bruszt, L. & McDermott, G. A. (2009) 'Transnational Integration Regimes as Development Programmes', in Bruszt, L. & Holzhacker, R. (eds) *The Transnationalization of Economies, States, and Civil Societies* (New York, Springer).

Buzogány, A. & Costa, O. (2009) 'Greening the Neighbourhood? The Environmental Dimension of the European Neighbourhood Policy in Morocco and Ukraine', *European Foreign Affairs Review*, 14, 4.

Casier, T. (2011) 'To Adopt or Not to Adopt: Explaining Selective Rule Transfer under the European Neighbourhood Policy', *Journal of European Integration*, 33, 1.

Christiansen, T., Petto, F. & Tonra, B. (2000) 'Fuzzy Politics Around Fuzzy Borders: The European Union's "Near Abroad"', *Cooperation and Conflict*, 35, 4.

Dawson, J. I. (1996) *Eco-nationalism: Anti-nuclear Activism and National Identity in Russia, Lithuania, and Ukraine* (Durham, NC, Duke University Press).

del Castillo, T. F. (2010) 'Revisiting the External Dimension of the Environmental Policy of the European Union: Some Challenges Ahead', *Journal for European Environmental & Planning Law*, 7, 4.

Dimitrov, V. (2009) *Cost of Institutional Harmonization in the ENP Countries* CASE Network Studies and Analyses No. 388/09 (Warsaw, Center for Social and Economic Research).

Dimitrova, A. (2010) 'The New Member States in the EU in the Aftermath of Accession. Empty Shells?', *Journal of European Public Policy*, 17, 1.

Dimitrova, A. & Dragneva, R. (2009) 'Constraining External Governance: Interdependence with Russia and the CIS as Limits to EU's Rule Transfer in Ukraine', *Journal of European Public Policy*, 16, 6.

Dupont, C. & Goldenmann, G. (2010) 'Convergence with the Water Framework Directive in the Context of the European Neighbourhood Policy', *elni review*, 6, 2.

Ehrke, A. (2010) *An Ever Cleaner Union? The Impact of European Environmental Measures in Poland and Ukraine* (Wiesbaden, VS Verlag).

European Commission (2003) *Convergence with EU Environmental Legislation in Eastern Europe, Caucasus and Central Asia: A Guide* (Brussels, European Commission).

European Commission (2010) *List of the EU–Ukraine Association Agenda Priorities for 2010—As Agreed by the Joint Committee at Senior Official's Level of EU–Ukraine Association Agenda on January 26, 2010* (Brussels, European Commission).

European Commission (2011) *Implementation of the European Neighbourhood Policy in 2010 Country Report on: Ukraine* COM (2011) 303 (Brussels, European Commission).

European Communities (2000) 'Directive 2000/60/EC of the European Parliament and of the Council of 23 October 2000 on Establishing a Framework for Community Action in the Field of Water Policy', *Official Journal* (OJ L327), 22 December, available at: http://eur-lex.europa.eu/LexUriServ/LexUriServ.do?uri=CELEX:32000L0060:EN:HTML, accessed 15 November 2012.

European Communities (2001) 'Directive 2001/42/EC of the European Parliament and of the Council on the Assessment of the Effects of Certain Plans and Programmes on the Environment', *Official Journal* (OJ L197), 27 June, available at: http://eur-lex.europa.eu/LexUriServ/LexUriServ.do?uri=CELEX:32001L0042:EN:HTML, accessed 15 November 2012.

Freyburg, T., Lavenex, S., Schimmelfennig, F., Skripka, T. & Wetzel, A. (2009) 'EU Promotion of Democratic Governance in the Neighbourhood', *Journal of European Public Policy*, 16, 6.

Friis, L. & Murphy, A. (1999) 'The European Union and Central and Eastern Europe: Governance and Boundaries', *Journal of Common Market Studies*, 37, 2.

Gawrich, A., Melnykovska, I. & Schweickert, R. (2010) 'Neighbourhood Europeanization through ENP: The Case of Ukraine', *Journal of Common Market Studies*, 48, 5.

GWP (2010) *Ukraine: Assessment of the Draft National Targeted Program for Water Management Development up to 2020* (Kyiv, Global Water Partnership).

Haas, E. B. (1964) *Beyond the Nation-State. Functionalism and International Organization* (Stanford, CA, Stanford University Press).

Hofer, S. (2008) *Die Europäische Union als Regelexporteur: Die Europäisierung der Energiepolitik in Bulgarien, Serbien und der Ukraine* (Baden-Baden, Nomos).

ICPS (2007) *Free Trade between Ukraine and the EU: An Impact Assessment* (Kyiv, International Centre for Policy Studies).

Kelley, J. (2006) 'New Wine in Old Wineskins: Promoting Political Reforms through the New European Neighbourhood Policy', *Journal of Common Market Studies*, 44, 1.

Keohane, R. O. & Nye, J. S. (1989) *Power and Interdependence* (Glenview, IL, Scott, Foresman).

Knill, C. & Tosun, J. (2009) 'Hierarchy, Networks, or Markets: How Does the EU Shape Environmental Policy Adoptions Within and Beyond its Borders?', *Journal of European Public Policy*, 16, 6.

Korppoo, A. & Moe, A. (2008) 'Joint Implementation in Ukraine: National Benefits and Implications for Further Climate Pacts', *Climate Policy*, 8, 3.

Kravchenko, S. (2010) 'Procedural Rights as a Crucial Tool to Combat Climate Change', *Georgia Journal of International and Comparative Law*, 38, 3.

Langbein, J. (2010a) 'À la carte-Die Ukraine und der Freihandel mit der EU', *Osteuropa*, 2, 4.

Langbein, J. (2010b) *Patterns of Transnationalization and Regulatory Change beyond the EU: Explaining Cross-Sectoral Variation in Ukraine*, unpublished PhD thesis, European University Institute, Florence

Lavenex, S. (2004) 'EU External Governance in "Wider Europe"', *Journal of European Public Policy*, 11, 4.

Lavenex, S. & Schimmelfennig, F. (2009) 'EU Rules Beyond EU Borders: Theorizing External Governance in European Politics', *Journal of European Public Policy*, 16, 6.

Lavenex, S. & Wichmann, N. (2009) 'The External Governance of EU Internal Security', *Journal of European Integration*, 33, 1.

Lindberg, L. N. (1963) *The Political Dynamics of European Economic Integration* (Stanford, CA, Stanford University Press).

Melnykovska, I. & Schweickert, R. (2008) 'Bottom-up or Top-down: What Drives the Convergence of Ukraine's Institutions towards European Standards?', *Southeast European and Black Sea Studies*, 8, 4.

Mendoza-Wilson, J. & Skarshevskiy, V. (2011) 'Climate Change and Energy Policies Global Trends— Ukrainian Response', presentation at the *3rd UN Climate Change Summit*, Kyiv, 23 March, available at: www.scm.com.ua/en/archive/download/24, accessed 20 September 2011.

O'Brien, T. (2010) 'Problems of Political Transition in Ukraine: Leadership Failure and Democratic Consolidation', *Contemporary Politics*, 16, 4.

Peters, G. (2005) 'Policy Instruments and Policy Capacity', in Painter, M. & Pierre, J. (eds) *Challenges to State Policy Capacity: Global Trends and Comparative Perspectives* (Basingstoke, Palgrave Macmillan).

Petkova, N., Stanek, R. & Bularga, A. (2011) *Medium-term Management of Green Budget: The Case of Ukraine* OECD Environment Working Papers, 31 (Paris, OECD Environment Directorate).

Popescu, N. (2010) *EU Foreign Policy and Post-soviet Conflicts: Stealth Intervention* (Abingdon, Routledge).

RAC (2009) *Assessment of the EU–Ukraine Action Plan Implementation: Environment and Sustainable Development* (Lviv, Resource and Analysis Center Society and Environment).

RAC (2011) *Otsinka vplivu na dovkillya v Ukrayini: Vyrishennya problemi po-evropeiski* (Lviv, Resource and Analysis Center Society and Environment), available at: http://www.rac.org.ua/fileadmin/user_ upload/documents/ppapers/OVD.Rezjume.pdf, accessed 15 November 2012.

Schimmelfennig, F. & Sedelmeier, U. (2004) 'Governance by Conditionality: EU Rule Transfer to the Candidate Countries of Central and Eastern Europe', *Journal of European Public Policy*, 11, 4.

Sedelmeier, U. (2008) 'After Conditionality: Post-accession Compliance with EU Law in East Central Europe', *Journal of European Public Policy*, 15, 6.

Stavcuk, I. (2008) 'Ukraine: Doppelter Klimawandel Treibhausgase senken, Wissen vermehren', *Osteuropa*, 58, 4–5.

Stegny, O. (2002) *Suchasni problemi ekologichnogo ruhu v Ukraini. Analitichniy zvit* (Kyiv, MAMA-86).

Stewart, S. (2009) 'NGO Development in Ukraine since the Orange Revolution', in Besters-Dilger, J. (ed.) *Ukraine on Its Way to Europe: Interim Results of the Orange Revolution* (Frankfurt, Peter Lang).

Stulberg, A. N. & Lavenex, S. (2007) 'Connecting the Neighbourhood: Energy and Environment', in Weber, K., et al., (eds), (2007).

Tsebelis, G. (2002) *Veto Players: How Political Institutions Work* (Princeton, NJ, Princeton University Press).

UCIPR (2010) *The 2nd Interim Report by the Civil Society's Monitoring of Implementation of EU–Ukraine Association Agenda Priorities (July–October 2010)* (Kyiv, Ukrainian Center for Independent Political Research).

UCIPR (2011) *The 3rd Interim Report by the Civil Society's Monitoring of Implementation of EU–Ukraine Association Agenda Priorities 2011* (Kyiv, Ukrainian Center for Independent Political Research; Institute for Economic Research and Policy Consulting; Center for Political and Legal Reforms).

UNDP Ukraine (2007) *National Environmental Policy of Ukraine: Strategic Evaluations and Recommendations* UNDP/GEF project National Capacity Self-Assessment for Global Environment Management in Ukraine (Kyiv, United Nations Development Programme).

UNECE (2007) *Environmental Performance Reviews Ukraine, Second Review* (New York & Geneva, United Nations Economic Commission for Europe).

Vachudová, M. A. (2007) 'Trade and the Internal Market in the EU's European Neighborhood Policy', in Weber, K., et al., (eds), (2007).

Vogel, D. & Kagan, R. A. (2004) *Dynamics of Regulatory Change: How Globalization Affects National Regulatory Policies* (Los Angeles, CA, University of California Press).

Weber, K., Smith, M. E. & Baun, M. (eds) (2007) *Governing Europe's Neighbourhood* (Manchester, Manchester University Press).

Wetzel, A. (2010) 'Umweltschutz und Bürgerbeteiligung. Chancen und Grenzen der Aarhus-Konvention in der Ukraine', *Osteuropa*, 60, 2–4.

Wilson, A. (2005) *Virtual Politics: Faking Democracy in the Post-Soviet World* (New Haven, CT, Yale University Press).

Wolczuk, K. (2009) 'Implementation without Coordination: The Impact of EU Conditionality on Ukraine under the European Neighbourhood Policy', *Europe-Asia Studies*, 61, 2.

Wolczuk, K. (2010) 'Convergence without Finalité: EU Strategy towards Post-Soviet States', in Henderson, K. & Weaver, C. (eds) *The Black Sea Region and EU Policy* (Farnham, Asghate).

WWF & HBS (2009) *Greening the European Neighbourhood Policy. A Handbook to Assess Implementation of the Action Plans in the Field of the Environment* (Brussels, World Wildlife Foundation for Nature and Heinrich Böll Stiftung).

Youngs, R. (2009) 'A Door Neither Closed nor Open: EU Policy towards Ukraine during and since the Orange Revolution', *International Politics*, 46, 4.

Zaharchenko, T. (2010) *On the Way to Transparency: A Comparative Study on Post-Soviet States and the Aarhus Convention* (Washington, DC, Woodrow Wilson International Center for Scholars).

Unpacking the Russian and EU Impact on Policy Change in the Eastern Neighbourhood: The Case of Ukraine's Telecommunications and Food Safety

JULIA LANGBEIN

Abstract

Russia is usually considered as being obstructive to European integration in the EU's Eastern neighbourhood, while the EU is portrayed as being the key promoter of convergence with EU rules. Thus, strong economic dependence on Russia and EU active leverage should account for cross-policy variation in convergence with EU rules. By comparing convergence in Ukraine's telecommunications and food safety regulations, I show that active leverage exerted by Western European multinationals rather than by the EU accounts for divergent outcomes. Further, Russia's 'bad guy' image does not hold if we stop treating Russia as a unitary actor but distinguish between passive and active leverage exerted by Russian government policies, the Russian market and Russian multinationals investing in the Eastern neighbourhood countries on domestic policy choices.

THE EUROPEAN UNION (EU) IS WIDELY PORTRAYED AS BEING the key external actor promoting convergence with EU rules in the Eastern neighbourhood countries (Lavenex 2008; Wolczuk 2008; Gawrich *et al.* 2010). The EU pursues a particular concept of convergence by which the Eastern neighbourhood countries are expected to unilaterally converge towards the EU model (European Commission 2004a, 2008). Considering that a large misfit between national and EU policy practices and institutional arrangements is characteristic for these countries, convergence with EU rules requires policy change in the Eastern neighbourhood countries (for explanations of different forms of misfit, see the Introduction to this collection). Students of the European neighbourhood conceive the EU's 'active leverage' (Vachudova 2005)—the deliberate application of conditionality, provision of assistance or facilitation of lesson-drawing through regulatory networks—as necessary to mitigate high adaptational costs for domestic actors in the Eastern neighbourhood countries (Weber *et al.* 2007; Freyburg *et al.* 2009; Gawrich *et al.* 2010).

I thank Esther Ademmer, Tanja A. Börzel, and Milada A. Vachudova as well as the two anonymous reviewers for their insightful comments. The usual disclaimer applies. Preparation of this essay was facilitated by the European University Institute in Florence and the Kolleg-Forschergruppe (KFG) 'The Transformative Power of Europe', hosted at the Freie Universität Berlin and funded by the German Research Council (*Deutsche Forschungsgesellschaft*).

By contrast, Russia is considered to be an 'alternative hegemon' in the region (Levitsky & Way 2005). The few studies that deal with Russia's policy towards the Eastern neighbourhood countries usually treat Russia as a unitary actor that is obstructive to European integration in its 'near abroad' (Sushko 2008; Haukkala 2009; Popescu & Wilson 2009). Some scholars, however, specify that the EU's Eastern neighbours are less likely to take on EU rules in policy fields where economic dependence on Russia in terms of investments or trade relations is high (Dimitrova & Dragneva 2009, pp. 854, 866). Considering the notion of 'business capture' that has characterised the relationship between the Russian state and business since Putin's first presidency in 1999 (Yakovlev 2006), Russian investments in the Eastern neighbourhood countries or close trade relations with Russia imply an extension of Russia's power politics aimed at limiting the EU's policy extension in the region (Sushko 2008; Dimitrova & Dragneva 2009, p. 866; Popescu & Wilson 2009).

The Ukrainian case, however, shows that active leverage exercised by the EU on policy change and economic dependence on Russia cannot account for cross-policy variation in convergence with EU rules. I argue that partial convergence with EU rules is even likely under conditions of high economic dependence on Russia and in the absence of EU efforts to promote policy change. To achieve at least partial convergence under these conditions some external actors must benefit from convergence and thus empower domestic reform coalitions. These external actors are typically multinational companies, including Russian ones. While the literature on Europeanisation and domestic change refers to active leverage in relation to the EU (Vachudova 2005; Haughton 2007), I apply this concept to non-state actors who can empower domestic reform coalitions by employing the same mechanisms as the EU. I argue that multinationals operating in Ukraine exercise active leverage on policy change through conditionality and lesson-drawing in policy sectors where convergence with EU rules increases their competitiveness on the Ukrainian or international markets. In this sense, my study reveals that active leverage exercised by multinationals rather than the EU can account for cross-policy variation in convergence with EU rules.

Further, I argue that both the EU and Russia can affect convergence with EU rules in the Eastern neighbourhood countries by exercising passive leverage. More precisely, they shape the incentives of Ukrainian state regulators and firms in a particular policy sector thanks to the attraction of their markets. They can also pursue certain policies that are not directly aimed at impinging on convergence with EU rules in Ukraine but still indirectly shape domestic incentives to pursue certain policies over others.[1] Contrary to conventional wisdoms, I show that the passive leverage exercised by the EU or the EU single market on policy change in the Eastern neighbourhood countries must not necessarily increase domestic incentives for convergence with EU rules. It can also make the application of EU rules less attractive. The same holds true for passive leverage exercised by Russian government policies or the Russian market.

I illustrate my argument by analysing Ukraine's convergence with EU rules in telecommunications and food safety regulations in the dairy industry from the mid-1990s to 2010.[2] I examine convergence in terms of rule adoption—the transposition of EU legislation

---

[1]See also Ademmer and Börzel, in this collection.

[2]This starting point for the analysis was chosen because Ukraine and the EU formally signed their Partnership and Cooperation Agreement (PCA), the first official agreement between both parties to envisage the approximation of Ukrainian legislation to the EU *acquis*, in 1994.

into national law, and behavioural compliance with EU rules.[3] While food safety regulations in Ukraine's dairy sector did not converge with EU rules resulting in complete inertia, Ukraine's telecommunications sector is characterised by partial convergence with EU rules by 2010 (European Commission 2009; European Commission & High Representative of the Union for Foreign Affairs and Security Policy 2011). In 2003 and 2004, the Ukrainian parliament adopted certain laws bringing the regulation of the telecommunications sector more in line with EU requirements (European Commission 2005, 2006). As a result, Ukraine established an independent national telecoms regulator that is supposed to fulfil almost the same regulatory tasks as its counterparts on the EU single market, but which lacks enforcement power (European Commission 2009).

Ukraine is an interesting case to examine how the EU and Russia have shaped cross-policy variation in convergence with EU rules. Ukraine's longstanding EU membership aspirations and its highly institutionalised relationship with the EU, if compared to other Eastern neighbours, should make the application of the EU's active leverage more likely.[4] If this study can show that Ukraine converges with EU rules despite the fact that the EU does not exercise active leverage, similar dynamics can be expected in other Eastern neighbours.[5] At the same time, Ukraine is one of Russia's closest neighbours in the Eastern neighbourhood countries and is one of the main targets of Russian expansionist ambitions in the post-Soviet space (Fischer 2007; Larrabee 2010). If the findings of this essay reveal that Russia plays a much more nuanced role in Ukraine than its 'bad guy' image suggests, we can expect similar results in other Eastern neighbourhood countries.

Students of Russia's impact on policy change in Ukraine usually focus on the energy sector. They argue that Russia's political leadership uses Russian investments in Ukraine's energy sector as well as its dependence on Russian energy imports to undermine Ukraine's economic integration with the EU (Dimitrova & Dragneva 2009; Popescu & Wilson 2009). Most often, insights from the energy sector inform claims about Russia's constraining impact on convergence in other policy sectors.[6] In contrast, I compare convergence with EU rules in two trade-related policy sectors: Ukraine's telecommunications and food safety regulations in the Ukrainian dairy industry. By comparing two policy sectors where the share of Russian investments varies significantly, I control for the impact of Russian investments on policy change in Ukraine. I find that convergence with EU rules is more progressive in Ukraine's telecommunications sector than in its dairy sector despite a stronger presence of Russian investors in the former.

The conventional wisdom: good guy EU, bad guy Russia

My comparative study of convergence with EU rules in Ukraine's telecommunications and food safety regulations challenges three conventional wisdoms concerning the EU's and Russia's impact on policy change in the Eastern neighbourhood countries, as discussed below.

---

[3]See Börzel and Langbein, in this collection.

[4]Ukraine was the first country among the Eastern neighbours to sign a PCA with the EU as early as 1994. Furthermore, the country was among the first ones to negotiate an Action Plan with the EU in early 2005 in the context of the European Neighbourhood Policy and the first among the Eastern neighbours to negotiate a Deep Free Trade Agreement with the EU in 2008.

[5]See also Ademmer and Börzel, in this collection.

[6]For a similar observation see Vahtra (2007).

The EU as the key promoter of convergence with EU rules in the Eastern neighbourhood countries?

While early research on the European Neighbourhood Policy (ENP) considered the prospects for convergence with EU rules as gloomy given the absence of an EU membership perspective, more recent accounts provide a more nuanced assessment and find a great deal of variation in convergence across countries and policy sectors (Lavenex & Schimmelfennig 2009; Gawrich *et al.* 2010; Langbein 2011; Börzel & Pamuk 2012). If the EU's Eastern neighbours align with EU rules, scholars interpret this outcome as an instance of 'Neighbourhood Europeanisation' (Gawrich *et al.* 2010; Börzel & Pamuk 2012), as a result of the EU's active leverage. Thus, the EU is widely perceived as the key promoter of convergence with EU rules.

The mechanisms that the EU uses to exercise active leverage on policy change in the Eastern neighbourhood countries have been discussed in-depth elsewhere (Börzel 2010; Langbein 2011; Langbein & Wolczuk 2012). Some students of the ENP emphasise that the EU applies policy-specific conditionality by linking rewards with the fulfilment of specific criteria.[7] As Gawrich *et al.* (2010) detail, access to the EU single market or trade liberalisation is likely to facilitate policy change in economic fields, while visa facilitation is considered as being the main reward to promote convergence in Justice and Home Affairs. Further, the EU provides the ENP partner countries with assistance through the transfer of knowledge, technologies or financial resources and thereby increases domestic capacities for policy change (Börzel 2010). Finally, Freyburg *et al.* (2009) argue that the setup of regulatory networks through which the EU promotes the *acquis* is likely to facilitate policy change. Regulators from EU neighbouring countries will become more aware of domestic policy problems and may start searching for new solutions through 'lesson-drawing' (Rose 1991; Slaughter 2004). Indeed, a few scholars have started to study convergence with EU rules in specific policies. With regard to explaining cross-policy variation in convergence with EU rules, they found that the EU applies its 'toolbox' with some success to empower reform-minded actors in some policy sectors but not in others (Freyburg *et al.* 2009; Gawrich *et al.* 2010).

In contrast, in the two policy sectors under scrutiny here, the EU does not exercise active leverage. The EU does not apply conditionality by linking policy-specific rewards to convergence. As far as food safety is concerned, the EU single market remains closed to dairy imports from Ukraine even if producers take on European food safety standards (European Commission 2008; EESC 2010). In telecommunications, the EU propagates the creation of independent regulators in the Eastern neighbourhood countries (European Commission 2004a, p. 19).[8] The EU does not tie convergence in telecommunications to any policy-specific rewards. Further, the EU has not set up a single assistance programme to promote convergence with EU rules either in telecommunications or in food safety.[9] Finally, the EU has not set up regulatory networks in either of the two policy sectors to promote convergence with EU rules. Despite the absence of active leverage of the EU, we however observe diverse outcomes in Ukraine's telecommunications and food safety regulations.

[7]See Ademmer and Börzel, in this collection; see also Langbein and Wolczuk (2012).

[8]In the PCA between the EU and Ukraine both parties agreed to cooperate with regard to the creation 'of an appropriate regulatory basis for the provision of telecommunicational ... services ...' (PCA 1998, Article 66). EU law stipulated the separation of ownership and regulation (Thatcher 2004).

[9]The EU assistance programmes in the field of food safety only focused on achieving compliance with the WTO SPS Agreement.

This suggests that the EU can hardly be the key promoter of convergence with EU rules in Ukraine.

Does Russia's political leadership constrain convergence with EU rules?

Theoretical accounts of Europeanisation note that convergence with EU rules is likely to be constrained under conditions of cross-conditionality, when other external actors link benefits for target countries to the fulfilment of conditions that differ from those of the EU (Schimmelfennig & Sedelmeier 2005, p. 15). In this sense students dealing with Russia's role in the EU's Eastern neighbourhood usually underline the intention of Russia's political leaders to undermine convergence with EU rules (Fischer 2007; Haukkala 2009; Popescu & Wilson 2009). As Fischer (2007, p. 20) details, 'Moscow increasingly uses economic power in order to exert political leverage and counterbalance disliked domestic developments in these states [Ukraine, Georgia, Moldavia]'. Further, Fischer (2007, pp. 20–21) notes that Russia conceives of the EU 'not exclusively as a partner but rather as the most important competitor in the struggle for influence in the post-Soviet space'.

Since the Russian market regulates its economic activities predominantly through non-Western regulatory institutions, students of the post-Soviet space often counter Russian-led regional initiatives to establish a common economic space among the Commonwealth of Independent States (CIS) with scepticism. They suspect Russia's political leaders maintain these institutions in order to simplify economic and political penetration of the CIS and to constrain economic integration with the EU (Shapovalova 2006; Sushko 2008). This fear is not groundless taking into account that Russian political leaders consider convergence with EU rules as 'potentially harmful and undermining Russia's other economic projects in the post-Soviet space' (Haukkala 2009, p. 5). Students of Russia's role in the EU's Eastern neighbours would expect Russia's political leadership to exercise 'active leverage' in order to undermine convergence with EU rules.

Yet, the Russian state lacks an adequate institutional framework to apply policy-specific conditionality, provide assistance or promote lesson-drawing by engaging domestic actors in regulatory networks. In theory, Russia could use the Single Economic Space (SES) with Ukraine, Kazakhstan and Belarus, which Ukraine joined in 2003, to tie rewards to the adoption and implementation of specific rules and norms that are not complementary with EU rules. However, Russia does not define common market rules that SES members must adopt and implement in their national context (Dimitrova & Dragneva 2009). In practice, Russian–Ukrainian relations within the SES do not go beyond the free trade agreement that both parties concluded as early as 1993 and which foresees tariff-free exports and imports in commodities such as machinery and dairy products. Further, the Russian state did not manage to set up a national aid agency for the CIS and has so far not set up any regulatory networks that could provide a platform for lesson-drawing among Ukrainian regulators in telecommunications or food safety (Langbein 2010).

Russian investments in the Eastern neighbourhood countries as an extension of Russian power politics?

Finally, students of Russia's role in the Eastern neighbourhood countries often interpret the activities of Russian multinationals as an extension of Russia's power politics. Students of

Russia's role in the EU's Eastern neighbourhood rarely distinguish between Russia's political leadership and Russian business. Most studies deal with Russia's impact in the fields of energy where state-owned Russian firms, like Gazprom or Rosneft, establish business networks with those in power in the Eastern neighbourhood countries, thereby limiting the EU's policy extension (Vahtra 2005, 2007; Dimitrova & Dragneva 2009, p. 866). Insights from the energy sector are often used to make general claims about Russian investments in Ukraine as a means of Russia's political leadership to slow down Ukraine's turn to the West (Shapovalova 2006; Sushko 2008). From this perspective, convergence with EU rules should hardly progress in Ukrainian telecommunications since Russian mobile operators have constantly held about 60% of Ukraine's network market from 2002 to 2008 (Blyakha 2009). By contrast, Russian investors have only controlled between 25% and 30% of the Ukrainian dairy market since 2003 (Libman & Kheifets 2006; Strubenhoff *et al.* 2007). Since Ukraine's convergence with EU rules in telecommunications has progressed faster than in the dairy sector, the share of Russian investments in a particular sector cannot account for diverse outcomes.

The argument: passive and active EU and Russian leverage shaping policy change in the Eastern neighbourhood

By drawing upon Vachudova (2005) I distinguish between passive and active leverage of external actors on domestic policy choices. By passive leverage I mean the attraction of foreign markets such as the European or Russian market as well as political decisions of the EU and Russian government authorities that did not aim at shaping convergence with EU rules in the Eastern neighbourhood countries, but indirectly shape the incentives of firms and/or state regulators in the Eastern neighbourhood countries to pursue certain policies over others. Active leverage entails the deliberate application of conditionality, provision of assistance and facilitation of lesson-drawing by external actors to influence convergence with EU rules. Both passive and active leverage can shape the incentives or capacities of firms and state regulators in the Eastern neighbourhood countries for pursuing particular policy choices, here supporting or hindering convergence with EU rules.

The case studies in this essay show that multinational companies, including Russian ones, exercise active leverage to foster convergence with EU rules in the Eastern neighbourhood countries in policy sectors where this increases their competitiveness on the Ukrainian or on international markets. For example, Western European and Russian multinationals are likely to promote convergence with EU rules on the Ukrainian market where their application undermines rent-seeking behaviour of powerful domestic actors such as the local government or local businessmen. In this sense, Western European and Russian multinationals empower domestic reform coalitions through financial and technical assistance or by facilitating lesson-drawing in regulatory networks in some policy sectors but not in others, thereby contributing to cross-policy variation in convergence with EU rules. My argument dovetails with findings of students of EU enlargement, who have emphasised the active role that (Western European) multinationals played in promoting EU rules in East European markets through the application of stricter (EU) standards and investments in local upgrading (Andonova 2003; Dries & Swinnen 2004). However, only a few scholars have stressed that Russian investors in the Eastern neighbourhood countries outside the energy sector do not necessarily follow political but simply market-oriented motivations (Vahtra 2007; Filippov 2010; Panibratov 2010). Russian multinationals in private ownership, which dominate less politicised sectors like telecommunications or food, are most likely interested in gaining new markets and customers which 'does not mean that they receive instructions for daily operations from the high ranks of power' (Vahtra 2007, p. 25).

The EU or the Russian government do not exercise active leverage by the deliberate application of conditionality, provision of assistance or facilitation of lesson-drawing. However, the attractiveness of the EU or Russian market, as well as EU policies or Russian government policies which are not aimed at directly promoting or undermining convergence with EU rules in the Eastern neighbourhood countries, can still increase the incentives of domestic state regulators or firms in the neighbourhood countries to pursue certain policies over others. In this sense, the EU's passive leverage does not necessarily create an incentive structure that facilitates convergence with EU rules. For instance, the level of protectionism characterising a particular sector on the EU internal market can decrease Ukrainian incentives to support the adoption of and behavioural compliance with EU rules (for explanations of different forms of compliance, see the Introduction to this collection.) In a similar vein, Russia's passive leverage does not necessarily produce an incentive structure that countervails convergence with EU rules in the Eastern neighbourhood countries but can also contribute to policy change in a particular sector.[10] While the presence of the Russian market as an alternative export destination can undermine convergence with EU rules, import bans imposed by Russian authorities on certain Ukrainian products can indirectly facilitate convergence.

Partial convergence in Ukrainian telecommunications

EU demands

In the field of telecommunications, the EU–Ukraine PCA puts emphasis on the creation of an 'appropriate regulatory basis for the provision of telecommunicational … services and for the use of radio frequency spectrum' (PCA 1998, Article 66). By the mid-1990s, the EU had constituted a supranational sectoral regime in telecommunications that prohibited member states from maintaining legal monopolies on supply and obliged them to promote competition. The major goal was to separate ownership from regulatory tasks in order to allow for unbiased and fair competition by preventing discrimination and facilitating access for all suppliers to services. While there is no single piece of EU legislation that explicitly requires the establishment of national regulatory authorities independent from the government, several EU Directives have promoted their creation by stipulating the separation of ownership and regulation.[11] Ukraine formally adopted most EU telecommunications rules in 2002 and 2004. The EU–Ukraine Action Plan, which both parties signed in 2005, underlines the need to implement these laws (European Commission 2005, Action 58).

Ukraine's telecommunications regulations in the mid-1990s

In the mid-1990s, Ukraine's regulatory approach in the telecommunications sector was not based on the regulation of competition, as on the EU single market, but on the protection of

[10]See also Ademmer and Börzel, in this collection.
[11]See Thatcher (2004) and European Communities (1997).

the (state-owned) supplier. In the mid-1990s, Ukraine's State Committee on Communications and Information (SCC), which was subordinated to the Ministry of Transport and Communications, regulated Ukraine's telecommunications sector and performed management functions within the state-owned operator Ukrtelekom, which covered 92% of the fixed-line market and all transmission facilities (Pazyuk 2006). Further, the SCC was in charge of licensing, tariffs, spectrum management and numbering, in clear contrast to EU laws which stipulated institutional structures where the central executive would delegate regulatory power to an independent national regulatory authority. Thus, the SCC was responsible for granting licenses for operators whose market entrance would endanger Ukrtelekom's monopoly position. Moreover, the responsibility for spectrum management allowed the SCC to allocate frequencies for both civil operators and the military. Since the range of frequencies determines the quality and operating range of telecom operators, the SCC was easily able to abuse its regulatory power in order to safeguard Ukrtelekom's monopoly position (Pazyuk 2006).

Domestic resistance to policy change until 1997

The regulatory approach that Ukraine pursued in the telecommunications sectors in the mid-1990s was fully compliant with preferences of the Ukrainian government. It allowed the state regulator SCC to protect state-owned Ukrtelekom, thereby keeping the company's market value high in view of its future privatisation. Unsurprisingly, the Ukrainian government lacked incentives to support convergence with EU telecommunications regulations. Until 1997, Ukraine's regulatory regime did not raise any concerns among telecommunications operators. The fixed line market was in the hands of state-owned Ukrtelekom whose management had obviously similar interests to the Ukrainian government and thus supported Ukraine's then regulatory approach. The mobile networks market was in the hands of a Ukrainian–Danish–Dutch–German consortium that owned the mobile operator Ukrainian Mobile Communications (UMC). Until 1997, UMC had a monopoly license from the Ukrainian government—one of the conditions demanded by UMC's foreign investors before concluding the joint venture (Abol'nikov 1997).[12] Given that Ukrtelekom (and therefore the Ukrainian state) held 51% of shares in the mobile operator UMC, the latter's Western management enjoyed privileged treatment from the SCC until its monopoly license expired in 1997. Until then, UMC had not met with any problems in obtaining licenses for inter-city connections, fixed lines and mobile services, and could easily regulate tariffs for interconnection with Ukrtelekom.[13]

UMC's preferential treatment stopped when the Ukrainian government did not prolong the monopoly license after 1997. More businesspeople, including those with personal ties to Ukrainian President Leonid Kuchma, wanted to make profits due to increasing demand for mobile services among Ukrainian consumers (Abol'nikov 1997; Primachenko 2002; Skibinskaya 2005). In 1997, a new mobile company called Kyivstar began its operations. Kyivstar was owned by the Norwegian mobile communications company Telenor (56.5%) and the Ukrainian company Storm (43.5%). Storm had direct personal links to President

---

[12]UMC was a joint venture between the incumbent operator Ukrtelekom, which held 51% of the shares, Tele Denmark Mobil (Denmark), Deutsche Telekom (Germany) and KPN (the Netherlands), which held 16% of shares each.

[13]Author's interview with Ukrainian expert (telecommunications), 21 September 2009, Kyiv.

Kuchma, as some of his family members occupied key management positions (Primachenko 2002; Skibinskaya 2005). Kyivstar's close personal ties with Kuchma spelled the end of the privileged treatment of the then market leader UMC by the SCC. Thanks to Kyivstar's fast access to licenses and smooth interconnection with Ukrtelekom, the company was quickly able to cover most of Ukraine's territory and thus attract more Ukrainian customers (Lisitsyn *et al.* 2005). By 2002, the UMC and Kyivstar companies held nearly 95% of the Ukrainian mobile networks market. Other newly formed mobile companies, such as the Ukrainian Digital Cellular Communication (DCC), had only minor market shares at that time.

Kyivstar had no interest in changing the regulation of Ukraine's telecommunications sector as it enjoyed unanimous support from the Ministry of Telecommunications and Transport thanks to the company's personal ties to President Kuchma. By contrast, UMC often had to wait for indefinite periods for responses from official bodies on the issue of licenses or interconnection with Ukrtelekom after the loss of its monopoly position (Bezborodov 2001). Faced with increasing competition from Kyivstar, UMC started to promote the establishment of an independent regulator which would protect UMC's interests by securing transparent and non-discriminatory access to licenses and interconnection services for all operators.

1997–2003: multinationals' active leverage empowers domestic reformers

Thus, from 1997 onwards, UMC began to diversify and empower domestic reformers by facilitating lesson-drawing in regulatory networks and the provision of technical and financial assistance in order to increase domestic support for convergence among Ukrainian policymakers and other private operators. When Russian mobile operator Mobile Telecommunications Systems (MTS) began to take over UMC in November 2002 and renamed the company MTS-Ukraine, the company's efforts to promote convergence with EU rules in Ukraine's telecommunications market continued as before. The Russian investor faced similar discrimination in terms of access to licenses and interconnections as its Western European predecessor and hoped to solve the problem by lobbying for an independent regulatory authority.

To begin with, in the late 1990s, UMC's Dutch management increasingly exposed their local staff, and particularly their legal experts, to European telecommunications regulations by promoting UMC's membership in the Global System for Mobile Communications Association (GSMA) Europe, a regulatory network for European mobile operators to exchange information and knowledge and coordinate lobbying activities.[14] In accordance with scholars arguing that the participation in regulatory networks facilitates lesson-drawing by changing the way local actors address policy problems at home (Rose 1991; Slaughter 2004; Freyburg *et al.* 2009), UMC's legal experts received updated information about recent trends and developments in European telecommunications regulation, allowing them to advise Ukrainian policymakers on possible legislative changes in Ukraine.[15]

---

[14]GSMA Europe is the biggest regulatory network of European mobile operators which represents around 147 operators serving around 558 million subscribers.

[15]Author's interview with Ukrainian mobile operator, 19 November 2008, Kyiv and with Ukrainian expert (telecommunications), 21 September 2009, Kyiv.

Further, UMC provided financial and technical assistance to identify potential reformers within the Ukrainian parliament and increase their capacities to enforce their claims. The operator started to lobby Ukrainian legislators through the US consulting company PBN in 2001 in order to attract support among government agencies and members of the Ukrainian parliament for a 'Law on Telecommunications' that would prescribe the establishment of an independent regulatory authority. PBN's staff managed to ally with MP Yurii Lutsenko, who was assigned to the parliamentary committee on telecommunications, and his assistant Olga Filippova. Lutsenko was a long-standing political opponent of President Kuchma and worked actively for Ukraine's European integration. Thus, he supported the drafting of a 'Law on Telecommunications' that would not only make it harder for the Kuchma regime to make profits by privileging the mobile operator Kyivstar and state-owned Ukrtelekom, but also bring Ukraine's legislation closer to European norms and standards (Ilgas 2002).

Lutsenko and Filippova managed to increase their capacities to enforce legislative changes thanks to the assistance provided by Western European and later Russian investors in Ukraine's telecommunications sector. In accordance with the interests of the mobile operator UMC, MP Lutsenko came up with a draft law, which was written by Filippova, consultants from PBN and UMC legal experts. The draft law was based on EC directives and regulations for the telecommunications sector and envisaged the establishment of a National Commission for Communications Regulations (NCCR) which would be institutionally and functionally separated from government authorities. To ensure the NCCR's financial independence, its budget should be comprised of operators' fees from licensing as well as by a special fee to be paid by operators, which would not exceed more than 0.03% of their annual income (Ilgas 2002).[16]

Around the same time, Ukraine's other mobile operators became increasingly dissatisfied with the regulation of Ukraine's telecommunications market. Kyivstar's relationship with Ukrainian President Kuchma became looser when Russian mobile operator Alfa-Telekom began to buy up major share packages from Kuchma's Storm company in summer 2002. Consequently, Kyivstar's Norwegian majority shareholder Telenor feared that Storm's withdrawal would result in the decline of Kyivstar's political power, which in turn spurred the company's management to look for solutions to regulatory matters other than personal ties to President Kuchma.[17] In a similar vein, Ukraine's third largest mobile operator DCC, which held 2% of the mobile networks market, became quickly dissatisfied with the preferential treatment of government authorities *vis-à-vis* the state-owned fixed-line monopolist Ukrtelekom. Around 2002, DCC's management sought to expand the operator's services across the Ukrainian territory and faced difficulties in buying new licenses and access to public networks.[18]

UMC successfully managed to channel both Kyivstar's and DCC's dissatisfaction with the regulation of Ukraine's telecommunications market into support for the establishment of an independent national regulatory authority by organising study tours to German and British telecom regulators for the managers and legal experts of Kyivstar, DCC and UMC.

---

[16]*Proekt zakonu pro telekommunikatsii*, 9 August 2002, available at: http://w1.c1.rada.gov.ua/pls/zweb_n/webproc4_1?id = &pf3511 = 12876, accessed 10 September 2011.

[17]Author's interview with European investor (telecommunications), 20 October 2008, Kyiv.

[18]Author's interviews with various Ukrainian and European experts and operators (telecommunications), 20 October 2008, 20 September 2009 and 16 October 2009.

Members of the parliamentary committee on telecommunications and their assistants were also invited to the study tours in order to increase support among legislators. Both Kyivstar's and DCC's management quickly understood that the establishment of an independent national regulatory authority would help them to improve the functioning of their services and facilitate market expansion.[19]

Multinationals combine forces: adoption of EU rules in 2003/2004

In summer 2002, Kyivstar and DCC approached MP Valeriy Pustovoitenko, the then head of the parliamentary committee on telecommunications. On the one hand, both operators wanted to ensure a majority for the draft law on telecommunications in the Ukrainian parliament. Considering that Pustovoitenko was the leader of the People's Democratic Party (*Narodno-Demokratychna Partiya*), which was also part of the pro-Kuchma bloc in the Ukrainian parliament, Lutsenko's faction strongly depended on Pustovoitenko's support for the draft law on telecommunications. One the other hand, Kyivstar and DCC lobbied Pustovoitenko to push through two important changes concerning Lutsenko's draft. Both operators wanted the NCCR to be completely funded by the Ukrainian budget. Further, NCCR's leadership should consist of seven instead of four commissioners, as foreseen by Lutsenko's draft, since the smaller operator DCC wanted to make sure that its representatives would find a place in the NCCR's leadership (Ilgas 2002). To gain Pustovoitenko's support, Lutsenko's faction agreed to these revisions (Galkovskaya 2002). In July 2003, Pustovoitenko and Lutsenko submitted a common draft law on telecommunications to the parliament and gained the majority of votes. President Kuchma signed the law a few months later (Kuksa 2003).

Shortly after the successful adoption of the Law on Telecommunications, MTS-Ukraine and Kyivstar once more joined forces in order to fully establish NCCR's independence. In summer 2003, they began to lobby for the revision of the existing law on 'Radio Frequency Resources' through MPs Lutsenko and Pustovoitenko. In accordance with EU rules, where the national regulatory authority has the impartial right to issue radio frequencies for military and civil use, the major demand of the mobile operators related to the transfer of regulatory power over spectrum management from the SCC to the NCCR. In the past, MTS-Ukraine had met with difficulty in acquiring the desired frequencies from the SCC (Yarovaya 2003). Kyivstar faced similar problems once Russian Alfa Telekom became its majority shareholder in March 2003 resulting in a loss of personal ties to President Kuchma. Both operators were extremely interested in acquiring 3G (UMTS) licenses[20] for which they would need more spectrum frequencies.

However, this time the MPs representing the interests of state-owned operator Ukrtelekom and the Ministry of Telecommunications had learned from their previous defeat regarding the Law on Telecommunications and engaged in an aggressive counter-lobbying campaign. Their main argument was that the transfer of responsibility for issuing radio frequencies for military usage to an independent regulator could endanger Ukraine's security in favour of the business interests of telecom operators. Due to the fact that many

---

[19]Author's interview with Ukrainian expert (telecommunications), 21 September 2009, Kyiv.

[20]Universal Mobile Telecommunications System (UMTS) is a third generation (3G) common standard in the mobile networks industry that allows operators to offer a wider range of services, such as video calling and high-speed internet connections.

MPs had occupied high-ranking posts in the army or the Ukrainian security service in the past, the Lutsenko–Pustovoitenko faction had to revise its draft law 'On Radio Frequency Resources' according to which the SCC would maintain control over the issue of radio frequencies for special military use, while the NCCR would only be in charge of issuing licenses for civil use.[21] In October 2004, the Ukrainian parliament adopted the revised law 'On Radio Frequency Resources' at the first reading. President Kuchma signed it shortly afterwards.[22]

Summing up, *de jure*, Ukraine's legislation in the telecommunications sector has been almost fully compliant with EU rules since 2003/2004. Only in the field of spectrum management does the NCCR lack the impartial right to issue licenses as prescribed by EU rules. Thus, convergence in terms of rule adoption has been achieved under the 'soft authoritarian' regime under President Kuchma, illustrating the limited extent to which regime type in Ukraine impacts policy change.[23] The progress made in Ukraine's telecommunications sector owes much to the previously described efforts of the two leading mobile operators in the Ukrainian market, Russian–Ukrainian MTS-Ukraine and Norwegian Kyivstar. They promoted convergence with EU telecommunications regulations by facilitating the participation of Ukrainian mobile operators in regulatory networks, which allowed for lesson-drawing. Further, Western European and Russian multinationals provided technical and financial assistance for domestic reformers.

Failed behavioural compliance with EU telecommunications regulations after 2004: the EU's passive leverage and the Orange Revolution

Despite the success of Western European and Russian multinationals in securing the adoption of major parts of EU telecommunications regulations resulting in the creation of an independent regulatory agency for Ukraine's telecommunications market in April 2005, the implementation of legislation turned out to be less successful. *De facto*, the regulatory power of the NCCR was heavily constrained. The chairman was changed frequently, particularly whenever a new government came into power. Moreover, given the NCCR's weak regulatory capacity, state-owned operator Ukrtelekom has often benefited from NCCR's decisions disproportionately in comparison to mobile operators. For instance, the state-owned operator Ukrtelekom was the only operator to receive a 3G license from the NCCR in August 2005 (Stepanchikov 2007).

The NCCR's decision was followed by harsh protests by MTS-Ukraine and Kyivstar which had applied for 3G licenses in November 2005 but were rejected by the NCCR. The mobile operators threatened to take the case to court since NCCR's regulatory policy violated existing Ukrainian legislation (Oliyarnyk 2005). Surprisingly, the two multi-national corporations did not make reference to Ukraine's violation of European norms and rules despite the country's commitment to 'establish the NCCR in accordance with the Law of Ukraine on Telecommunications' as noted in the EU–Ukraine Action Plan which was signed in early 2005 (European Commission 2005, p. 36). Thus, notwithstanding the upgraded scope and intensity of EU–Ukraine cooperation from 2005 onwards in the

---

[21]Author's interviews with various Ukrainian telecommunications experts, 20 November 2008, 21 September 2009 and 16 October 2009, Kyiv.

[22]*Zerkalo Nedeli*, 43, 518, 23–29 October 2004.

[23]See also Langbein and Wolczuk (2012).

framework of the ENP, the EU did not provide an opportunity structure for Western European and Russian multinationals operating on Ukraine's telecoms market to legitimise their criticism against the NCCR's decisions.

Interestingly, former opposition members, who had supported policy change in Ukraine's telecommunications in the early 2000s, had become part of the ruling elite after the Orange Revolution in 2004/2005. Despite their official pro-EU stance, they also did not criticise the lack of rule implementation. Ukrtelekom's profits totalled nearly $200 million in 2004, all of which went directly into the state budget (World Bank 2005). Furthermore, the state-owned operator was expected to create additional revenues in any future full or partial privatisation. Thus, Ukraine's new political leaders had similar interests in protecting Ukrtelekom to the previous Kuchma government.

While the adoption of EU compliant legislation took place under Kuchma's leadership, 'the democratic breakthrough' (Aslund & McFaul 2006) after the Orange Revolution did not facilitate the implementation of Ukraine's telecommunications legislation. In response to the critique raised by Kyivstar and MTS-Ukraine, the new Cabinet of Ministers under Prime Minister Yulia Timoshenko agreed to make the necessary spectrum available for the sale of 3G licenses to the two mobile giants. But nothing happened. When Kyivstar finally launched a lawsuit against the NCCR in March 2007, claiming that the regulatory body was obliged to issue licenses for the provision of 3G services as well as corresponding radio frequencies to Kyivstar according to Ukrainian law, the Cabinet of Ministers approved a national frequency distribution table allocating 70% of the radio spectrum for civil use. Owing to the financial crisis that hit Ukraine in autumn 2008, the Ukrainian government under Prime Minister Yulia Timoshenko was in urgent need of cash and decided to initiate an auction for 3G licenses in spring 2009 (Kornienko 2009).

But in October 2009, President Yushchenko blocked the transfer of the radio spectrum needed to use 3G licenses from military to civil use in a decree, in order 'to safeguard Ukraine's defensive capabilities'.[24] His protest was less motivated by an interest in protecting Ukrtelekom than by the long-standing political controversies with Prime Minister Timoshenko, who had announced she would run against him in the presidential elections of 2010 (Kornienko 2009). After the presidential intervention, Kyivstar and MTS-Ukraine declared that they would not participate in the auction due to the fact that the 3G licenses would be useless without the corresponding spectrum. The NCCR was forced to cancel the tender. It remains to be seen to what extent the recent privatisation of Ukrtelekom in March 2011[25] will increase the chances for the auction of 3G licenses. At the time of writing, the NCCR had not yet initiated such an auction.

The previous discussion suggests that the changed political landscape and the intensified cooperation between the EU and Ukraine in the framework of the ENP from 2005 onwards did not facilitate the implementation of EU rules on Ukraine's telecommunications market. These findings are counterintuitive to the initial expectations of students of Ukraine who expected greater progress after the Orange Revolution (Gromadzki *et al.* 2004; Lieven 2004) and intensified EU–Ukraine cooperation (Wolczuk 2008). Further, it is noteworthy

[24]*Reuters*, 21 October 2009.
[25]On 11 March 2011, the Ukrainian government sold 92% of Ukrtelekom's shares to the European Privatization and Investment Corporation (EPIC) based in Austria. At the time of writing it is not known whether EPIC's management acted on behalf of Ukrainian oligarchs or Russian or Turkish investors (Olearchuk 2011). EPIC denies these rumours (Shamota 2011).

that the EU did not exert active leverage to empower reform-minded domestic actors to take on EU rules despite respective statements in the PCA (1998), and the EU–Ukraine Action Plan (European Commission 2005). The EU did not provide knowledge transfer through trainings or seminars and did not promote the participation in regulatory networks, such as the European Regulators Group for Electronic Communications Networks and Services (ERG), which seeks to harmonise European telecoms regulation and solve common problems.[26]

The inactivity of the EU can be explained by the fact that the telecommunications sector was not among its priority issues as compared to other policy areas, such as technical standards, state aid or public procurement. Ukraine's mobile telecommunications sector developed rapidly despite the aforementioned *de facto* regulatory deficiencies. Mobile phone penetration has grown steadily in Ukraine, increasing from 42% at the end of 2004 to nearly 85% by September 2006 and rising to 119% as of January 2008 (Pazyuk 2006).[27] The EU presumably did not perceive any pressing need to support Ukraine in this area.[28]

Lack of Russian leverage

Interestingly, process tracing did not provide evidence for any active or passive leverage exerted by the Russian government or the Russian market. Russia's political leaderships did not promote a set of norms that would comply or contradict EU telecommunications regulations through capacity building, lesson-drawing or the application of cross-conditionality.[29] In a similar vein, the Russian government did not exert any passive leverage on policy change in Ukraine's telecommunications sector. None of the political decisions taken by the Russian government in the time period under scrutiny shaped the incentive structure of Ukrainian state actors, mobile operators or Western European or Russian investors in the telecommunications sector.

Inertia in Ukraine's food safety regulations

EU demands

Regulatory convergence in food safety concerns the harmonisation of specific safety standards for food products and of control systems to enforce manufacturers' compliance. The EU–Ukraine PCA foresees 'the gradual approximation of Ukrainian standards to Community technical regulations concerning … agricultural food products including sanitary and phytosanitary standards' (PCA 1998, Article 60). The EU–Ukraine Action Plan specifies the EU demands. The Action Plan seeks to achieve 'progress in convergence with EU food traceability legislation; general food safety principles and requirements;

[26]Membership in the ERG is limited to EU member states, but 'the Group may invite other experts and observers to attend its meetings' (European Commission 2002a, Article 5). This would thus also allow the body to invite regulators from neighbouring countries as observers.

[27]See also 'Demand for Mobile Services Rises as Market Saturates', *Kyivpost*, 21 February 2008. Market penetration over 100% means that subscribers use more than one operator.

[28]Author's interview with various Ukrainian telecommunications experts, 20 September 2008 and 20 November 2009, Kyiv.

[29]But see also Ademmer and Börzel, in this collection.

effectively implement the Hazard Analysis Critical Control Point (HACCP) system' (European Commission 2005, Action 32).

Hence, regulatory convergence with EU food safety regulations concerns two aspects: on the one hand, countries need to harmonise their national standards with EU food safety standards which prescribe, for example, testing procedures for antibiotics or particular hygiene practices (Garcia 2006; European Council 1993; European Commission 2004b). On the other hand, countries need to enforce the EU's regulatory approach which is based on the 'producer's primary responsibility' (European Commission 2002b). Accordingly, food and feed operators from farmers and processors to retailers and caterers must carry out their own checks and take samples to ensure the marketing of safe products based on the application of so-called HACCP principles (Giorgi & Lindner Friis 2009).[30] Thus, the instruments to ensure food safety rely first and foremost on 'enforced self-regulation' (Garcia 2006, p. 17) with the aim of ensuring food safety throughout the production process. Retailers operating on the EU market have increasingly developed private safety management schemes on the basis of HACCP principles. As a result, food producers in the EU often voluntarily certify compliance with private process standards of particular retailers through third-party certifiers (IFC 2009). Public authorities, in turn, must conduct inspections in order to check that HACCP plans are in place and that a monitoring system has been established by the operators (Wendler 2008).

Ukraine's food safety regulations in the mid-1990s

In the mid-1990s, Ukrainian food producers applied food quality and safety standards developed in the framework of the GOST standards (*Gossudarstvenny standart*)[31] system during the Soviet era. In contrast to European standards, GOST standards allowed the existence of certain substances in milk, or allowed higher amounts than the EU, and prescribed different testing methods. Furthermore, Ukraine applied different hygiene standards (Moody & Polivodsky 2004; Garcia 2006). Non-compliance with EU sanitary and phytosanitary standards (SPS) was thus significant, since Ukrainian GOST standards not only set different safety requirements than the EU's SPS, but include mandatory quality parameters. As a result, Ukrainian dairy producers were not allowed to export their products to the EU in the mid-1990s. In terms of the food safety control system, Ukraine's problem-solving approach to ensure food safety was based on prescriptive 'command and control' measures. Ukraine's state agencies were primarily engaged in testing end products. As mentioned earlier, the EU emphasised 'producers' primary responsibility' (Moody & Polivodsky 2004; IFC 2009).

Mid-1990s until 2006: EU and Russian passive leverage facilitate inertia

From the mid-1990s onwards, Ukraine's dairy sector witnessed a growing entrance of foreign investors. Between 1996 and 2007, several French dairy producers bought dairy processing plants in Ukraine. As a result, their market share in Ukraine's dairy market

---

[30]HACCP stands for Hazard Analysis and Critical Control Points. It forms a preventive food control system to address physical, chemical and biological hazards at different points of the food supply chain. In 1993, the EU mandated the application of HACCP principles for the first time (European Council 1993).

[31]The 'GOST standard' is an acronym for '*Gossudarstvenny standart*' which means state standard.

reached about 10% in 2006 and 12% by 2007 (Strubenhoff *et al.* 2007). By 2006, the share of Western European dairy processors in Ukraine's market had thus reached similar levels to those seen in Poland in 2003.

Some scholars have convincingly shown that foreign investment facilitated the upgrading of local dairy farms and regulatory reforms in Eastern Europe or Latin America (Reardon & Berdegué 2002; Dries & Swinnen 2004). However, Western European dairy producers operating in Ukraine did not invest in upgrading local milk standards to European requirements as they, for example, did in the Polish milk-producing sector. In contrast to their activities in Poland, Western European investors have rarely installed the technical equipment necessary for compliance at collection points, such as coolers. Further, they have not introduced free laboratory testing for antibiotics, nor have they provided credit to Ukrainian milk producing plants, which became part of their supply chains, for their compliance with EU milk standards. Western European investors have also failed to implement a safety management system based on HACCP principles, as prescribed by the EU, for their Ukrainian plants.

The inactivity of Western European dairy firms operating in Ukraine can be explained by the fact that the EU dairy market is not only strongly protected through high subsidies and import tariffs but also saturated due to high levels of self-sufficiency (109% in 2008).[32] The EU, or more precisely the EU single market, thus exercises passive leverage by creating an incentive structure for multinationals that countervails convergence with EU rules in Ukrainian dairy. Western European investors like Danone do not intend to export from Ukraine to the EU since their production plants operating in EU member states can fulfil the demands of the EU single market. Instead, these multinationals seek to enter new markets. They are interested in producing for the Ukrainian market or to export dairy products from Ukraine to Russia, where Western brands are still in the process of developing their market position. Unlike in the Ukrainian telecommunications sector where foreign investors promoted EU rules to increase their competitiveness *vis-à-vis* Ukrainian operators, Western European dairy producers lack similar incentives with regard to Ukraine's dairy sector. They, instead, apply GOST standards to ensure the quality and safety of their products, which date back to the Soviet Union and are still mandatory in Ukraine and in Russia.[33]

Russian investors, who entered the Ukrainian dairy market in 2003, followed similar business strategies to their Western European counterparts. Since their market entrance, the two leaders on the Russian dairy market, Unimilk and Wimm Bill Dann, have consistently controlled between 25% and 30% of the Ukrainian dairy market, and produce mainly for local consumption (Libman & Kheifets 2006; Strubenhoff *et al.* 2007). Their Ukrainian suppliers of raw milk also fail to meet EU safety requirements, and their processing plants do not monitor food safety based on HACCP principles.[34]

Ukrainian dairy producers, who accounted for about 65% of the local dairy market in 2006, give similar reasons for not investing in upgrading their production plants in order to

---

[32]Author's interviews with employees of Western European dairy company operating in Ukraine, 6 November 2008; Ukrainian food safety expert, Western donor organisation, 23 September 2008; and European food safety expert, 26 September 2008, Kyiv.

[33]Author's interviews with employees of Western European dairy company operating in Ukraine, 6 November 2008; and Ukrainian food safety expert, Western donor organisation, 26 September 2008, Kyiv.

[34]Author's interview with Ukrainian food safety expert, Western donor organisation, 26 September 2008, Kyiv.

become eligible for export to the EU market.[35] They are fully aware that the EU market does not depend on dairy imports from Ukraine. They understand that the application of European safety standards and the implementation of HACCP principles would not necessarily result in access to the EU single market given the high level of protectionism and self-sufficiency that characterises the EU dairy market.

Apart from the EU, Russia also exercises passive leverage and contributes to inertia in Ukraine's food safety regulations. As mentioned earlier, the Russian market accepts GOST standards. It is an alternative market for Ukrainian dairy products, thereby decreasing the incentives for Western European, Russian and Ukrainian dairy producers operating on the Ukrainian market to promote convergence with EU rules. Furthermore, Ukraine negotiated free trade agreements with Russia and other CIS countries after the break-up of the Soviet Union, that allow Ukrainian dairy products to access these markets without any tariff barriers.

Thus, it is not surprising that Ukrainian dairy producers sell 60% of their products on the Ukrainian market, while 40% are exported, mainly to Russia, the CIS and other countries that accept GOST standards (World Bank 2007). In contrast, the EU-27 became negligible as an export destination for Ukrainian dairy products after EU enlargement. From 2004 to 2007, the share of the EU-27 in Ukrainian dairy exports dropped from 2.8% to 0.9%. Ukraine only exports low value-added dairy products for non-human consumption, such as casein, to the EU, a sector where safety requirements are not as demanding (IFC 2009). Consequently, Russia's share in Ukrainian dairy exports has increased from 57% in 2001 to 71.7% in 2004, as shown in Table 1. High value-added products, such as cheese, constitute the bulk of Ukraine's dairy exports to Russia.

As far food safety is concerned, the costs of convergence did not exceed the benefits for Western European and Russian multinationals as well as Ukrainian dairy producers. Both, the EU and Russia exercised passive leverage that made it less beneficial for multinationals as well as Ukrainian dairy firms to promote the application of European food safety standards and to invest in upgrading production processes and teaching local staff how to monitor food safety on the basis of HACCP principles.

Russia's import ban in 2006 and the incentive structure for policy change

For the period between 2004 and 2007, Table 1 displays a steep decline in exports to Russia. This development is not a sign of Russia's decreasing importance as an export destination for Ukrainian dairy products, but was caused by a ban on dairy imports from Ukraine in early 2006. Officially, Russia's federal service for veterinary and phytosanitary surveillance, Rosselkhoznadzor, imposed the ban because Ukraine's dairy products did not comply with Russian food safety and quality standards. Yet, food safety experts interpreted the ban as a reaction to demands raised by Russian dairy producers with Rosselkhoznadzor, since the decline in imports from Ukraine led to a rise in prices in Russia.[36]

---

[35]Author's interviews with European food safety expert, 15 February 2008, and employees of Ukrainian dairy company, 16 October 2008, Kyiv.

[36]Author's interview with Ukrainian food safety expert, Western donor organisation, 14 October 2009, Kyiv. See also Kuksa (2006).

TABLE 1
UKRAINE'S DAIRY EXPORTS TO THE EU AND RUSSIA COMPARED TO THE REST OF THE WORLD BY
COMMODITY (2001, 2004 AND 2007)

	Total exports ($ million)			Of which exports to the EU-25 (%)			Of which exports to Russia (%)			Of which exports to the rest of the world*		
Year	2001	2004	2007	2001	2004	2007	2001	2004	2007	2001	2004	2007
Dairy	266	446	623	10.5	2.8	0.9	57.0	71.7	42.0	32.5	25.5	57.1

Note: *The majority of Ukraine's dairy exports go to the CIS and North Africa where GOST standards are accepted.
Source: Emerson *et al.*, (2006), Russian Federal Customs Service, State Statistics Committee of Ukraine, Eurostat, own calculations.

As a result of the ban, Russia's share in Ukraine's total dairy exports dropped to 32% in 2006 (Hess *et al.* 2008). During the first months of the ban, Ukrainian dairy producers suffered high financial losses since exports to Russia had totalled $391 million in 2005 (Vyse 2006). Consequently, they started to look for alternative markets, which explains why Ukraine's dairy exports to the 'rest of the world' almost tripled from $113 million in 2004 to $355 million in 2007 (Table 1). In particular, Ukraine increased its dairy exports to other CIS countries as well as Northern African countries where Ukrainian standards were accepted (Nivievskyi & von Cramon-Taubadel 2008).

Russia's import ban on Ukraine's dairy products changed the effects of the EU's and Russia's passive leverage on the policy choices of foreign and Ukrainian dairy producers. Some plants belonging to French, Russian and Ukrainian investors signalled greater interest in EU food safety standards since the Russian market was no longer an alternative export destination. These companies wanted to acquire the permission to export their products to the EU in order to send a positive message to the market by signalling that their products met European food standards (Gosudarskaya 2009).[37] By the force of the attraction of its standards, the EU's passive leverage increased domestic incentives for convergence with EU food safety standards and regulations. While the adoption and implementation of internationally acknowledged European food safety standards would not facilitate access to the (highly protected and saturated) EU dairy market, Russian, Western European and Ukrainian owners of dairy plants hoped to improve their image and thus increase the competitiveness of Ukrainian dairy products on the local and CIS markets.

Shortly after Russia had imposed the ban in January 2006, 17 Ukrainian dairy plants, of which the vast majority was in Ukrainian ownership, therefore requested the State Veterinary Office in Ukraine to invite inspectors from the Food and Veterinary Office (FVO)[38] of the Directorate General for Health and Consumer Affairs of the European Commission (Direction generals de Santé et Consommateurs, DG SANCO) to visit their plants and check their compliance with EU food safety regulations. However, only three out of 17 dairy plants, among them one owned by Russian investors, finally participated in the inspections that took place in summer 2008. The rest had underestimated the demands of the EU when they asked for FVO inspections in early 2006, and did not deem most of their

[37]Author's interviews with European food safety experts, 15 February and 15 October 2008, Kyiv.
[38]The FVO is in charge of monitoring compliance with EU food safety regulations within the European Union and in third countries exporting to the EU.

plants to be ready for inspection.[39] Furthermore, the competitive pressure on Ukrainian dairy plants, which had increased after Russia imposed its ban, decreased again over time, since Rosselkhoznadzor lifted the Russian import ban for an increasing number of Ukrainian dairy plants between April 2006 and summer 2008. The remaining three plants, which registered for the FVO inspections, were not deemed to be compliant with EU food safety standards by the European inspectors (European Commission 2009).[40] At the time of writing this essay, the situation had not changed. Dairy products from Ukraine are still not allowed to access the EU single market.[41]

Tracing (the lack of) active leverage

The previous discussion reveals the mixed effects of passive leverage exercised by the EU and Russia on policy change in Ukraine's food safety regulations. By contrast, the EU and Russia's political leadership have so far not exercised any active leverage through conditionality, capacity-building assistance or by facilitating lesson-drawing in regulatory networks to shape domestic policy choices.

With regard to conditionality, the EU does not tie any rewards to convergence with European food safety standards and regulations. Even if foreign investors or Ukrainian dairy producers would apply European standards, the EU would not open its market for Ukrainian products. Further, assistance programmes do not aim to promote European food safety rules. To be sure, the EU launched its first technical assistance projects in the area of food safety regulation in 2003 in reaction to Ukraine's growing interest in joining the World Trade Organization (WTO).[42] However, the projects aimed at bringing Ukraine's food safety legislation into line with WTO SPS requirements rather than with EU rules (Moody & Polivodsky 2004). Following the WTO SPS Agreement, the EU sought to ensure that Ukraine's legislation would prohibit any discrimination against foreign food imports (including dairy) and acknowledge international food standards and respective certificates at border controls (World Bank 2004). Hence, food imports cannot be obliged to comply with Ukrainian GOST standards. The adoption and implementation of these legislative provisions would not, however, result in higher levels of convergence with EU food safety regulations.

Apart from achieving compliance with the WTO SPS Agreement, the agenda of the EU project also foresaw that the EU's implementation of the SPS agreement should serve as a model and provide guidelines for the drafters of the law. In this respect, a project report written by the European experts stressed that Ukraine—as a non-EU candidate country—'had no obligation to implement measures that go beyond WTO SPS requirements' (Moody & Polivodsky 2004, p. 8). Instead, EU food safety principles should find their way into

[39]Author's interview with several European experts (food safety), 15 February and 23 September 2008, Kyiv.

[40]*ProUA*, 26 September 2008.

[41]Food and Veterinary Authority (FVO), Third country list of establishments, list per section, available at: https://webgate.ec.europa.eu/sanco/traces/output/non_eu_listsPerActivity_en.htm#, accessed 26 June 2012.

[42]Ukraine had applied for WTO membership as early as 1993, but due to the economic decline that hit the country throughout the 1990s, WTO accession and trade liberalisation took a back seat among the priorities of the Ukrainian government. When Ukraine's economy started to grow in 2000, WTO accession was put back on the political agenda (Garcia 2006). Author's interviews with EU official, DG Relex, 21 November 2008, and Ukrainian food safety expert, 14 October 2009, Kyiv.

Ukrainian legislation 'where feasible' (Moody & Polivodsky 2004, p. 9). These lines are somewhat contradictory to the formulations found in the EU–Ukraine PCA and the EU–Ukraine Action Plan, according to which both parties aim to bring Ukrainian food safety standards in line with Community legislation. Apparently, the European Commission had no real interest in forcefully promoting convergence with EU food safety regulations since Ukrainian products could easily increase the competition for European food products on world markets once Ukrainian producers applied internationally acknowledged standards. A statement made by one EU official is illustrative in this respect:

> The European Commission does not support private business in any third country since such a policy would promote market distortion and produce additional competition for European agri-food business, especially in a sector as vulnerable and highly protected as the European dairy sector. In contrast to candidate countries, which are expected to achieve mandatory compliance with the *acquis communautaire* and food safety requirements, Ukraine is not obliged to make all its companies compliant. It's Ukraine's choice to fulfil the requirements.[43]

In the absence of EU active leverage on Ukraine's convergence with EU food safety regulations, Ukraine's food law 'On the Quality and Safety of Food Products' (hereafter referred to as 'Ukraine's Food Law'[44]), which was drafted with the help of EU experts and adopted by the Ukrainian parliament in September 2005, foresaw non-discrimination against food imports applying international food safety standards rather than the adoption of EU rules for the regulation of the Ukrainian market. Further, the European experts recommended the implementation of some EU principles of food safety control, such as 'producers' primary responsibility'. This suggestion did not, however, find support among the state officials from the Ukrainian Ministries of Health and Agriculture although this would have increased convergence with EU rules. Similar to the case of Ukraine's telecommunications sector, the political changes after the Orange Revolution did not bring Ukraine's rules and norms closer to EU requirements. Ukraine's regulators had no incentive to prescribe the costly implementation of EU food safety regulations due to the lack of rewards. Instead, they decided to specify only the voluntary application of HACCP in Article 20 of Ukraine's Food Law. In fact, state regulators see the permission to voluntarily implement HACCP as a 'paper tiger' with no real impact for the regulatory powers of Ukrainian food safety authorities, since Ukrainian food operators will not implement HACCP on the domestic market given the lack of economic incentives (IFC 2009).[45]

Another component of the aforementioned EU assistance project targeted the Central State Laboratory of Veterinary Medicine (CSLVM), which is in charge of testing the quality of food products of animal origin, vegetables and animal feed. The EU provided the CSLVM with funds for new laboratory equipment and financed training for the local staff to conduct food quality controls to European standards according to a number of parameters. The CSLVM was eventually accredited for the testing of 50 parameters of quality and safety of animal products and forage by the German accreditation agency Deutsches Akkreditierungssystem Prüfwesen (DAP) (Garcia 2006). Nonetheless, the project's agenda

---

[43] Author's interview with EU official (DG Relex), 21 November 2008, Kyiv.

[44] The Law of Ukraine 'On the Quality and Safety of Food Products and Food Raw Materials', No. 2809-IV, 6 September 2005.

[45] Author's interview with state official, Central Veterinary Agency of Ukraine, 2 October 2008, Kyiv.

further confirms the fact that EU assistance did not aim at promoting convergence with EU rules. The EU's exclusive focus on state agencies is particularly surprising given that the EU food safety control system is based on public–private coordination. However, no assistance has been provided to producers or private certifiers in order to train them in how to implement and monitor European food safety standards and the HACCP principles. The current situation is highly beneficial for the CSLVM since it can now exploit its monopoly to extract bribes. State veterinary officers frequently ask local firms to pay extra fees for faster services or fewer inspections (IFC 2009). A food safety expert from one EU member state working in Ukraine comments on the EU assistance in the area of food safety regulation in the following manner:

> The European Commission has no clue about Ukraine's food safety system or is simply not interested in understanding and changing it [. . .]. Instead of strengthening private capacities for regulation needed to implement EU food safety rules, the EU spends money on the improvement of state laboratories, which keep the system of Soviet control, i.e. they control the producers and distributors.[46]

Finally, the EU has not facilitated the participation of Ukrainian regulators in regulatory networks on food safety, which could have fostered processes of 'lesson-drawing' among them. Ukraine's activity, or rather its inactivity, within the framework of the Codex Alimentarius Commission (CAC) is illustrative in this respect. The CAC of the United Nations (UN) is a multilateral organisation in charge of setting international (public) food standards. The Codex develops those standards, guidelines and recommendations upon which the WTO SPS Agreement, and internationally acknowledged food standards, including European ones, are based. The EU is also a member of the CAC. In this respect, participation in the Codex is likely to increase the understanding of participating regulators about international (and thus European) food standards, and can also equip them with the knowledge needed to develop standards at home. Notwithstanding the fact that Ukraine's National Commission for the Codex Alimentarius was created in 1999 to bring national food safety legislation into line with the standards proposed by Codex, Ukraine did not accede to the CAC until 2004. At the time of writing, the National Commission had not yet taken up its work.[47]

The previous analysis suggests that the EU and the Russian government did not exercise active leverage to shape domestic policy choices regarding convergence with EU rules in the field of food safety. Instead, the EU focused exclusively on preparing Ukraine for WTO membership in order to ensure that Ukrainian authorities would not discriminate against Western food imports. Facing a highly protected and self-sufficient EU dairy market, multinational investors in the Ukrainian dairy sector for their part were not inclined to promote regulatory convergence by investing in upgrading or the introduction of HAACP-based food control systems. Instead they produce for the local Ukrainian market or export their products to Russia and the CIS. Hence, none of the external actors employed mechanisms to increase domestic incentives and capacities for adopting and/or implementing EU food safety regulations in the Ukrainian dairy sector.

[46]Author's interview with European food safety expert advising the Ukrainian government, 14 November 2008, Kyiv.
[47]See IFC (2009).

Conclusion

The current literature on policy change in the EU's Eastern neighbourhood suggests that high economic dependence on Russia in terms of investments or trade relations constrains convergence with EU rules (Dimitrova & Dragneva 2009). While Russian investments in the Eastern neighbourhood countries are considered as an extension of the power politics of Russia's political leaders towards its 'near abroad', the presence of the Russian market decreases incentives of state regulators and firms in the Eastern neighbourhood countries to converge with EU rules as it offers an alternative export destination. By contrast, EU active leverage is widely seen as a necessary condition for convergence with EU rules in the Eastern neighbourhood countries.[48] This study makes two contributions to the scholarly debate about the impact of the EU and Russia on policy change in the Eastern neighbourhood countries by distinguishing between state and non-state actors, as well as between active and passive leverage.

First, this essay presents a more nuanced assessment of the Russian impact on policy change in the EU's Eastern neighbourhood.[49] I have shown that Russia's 'bad guy' image does not hold if we stop treating Russia as a unitary actor shaping convergence with EU rules in Ukraine. The current debate is predominantly informed by insights from the energy sector where Russia's political leadership has exercised active leverage to constrain convergence with EU rules in Ukraine and other Eastern neighbourhood countries (Vahtra 2007; Sushko 2008; Dimitrova & Dragneva 2009). However, we should be cautious to draw inferences about its role in trade-related policy sectors like telecommunications or food safety.

I have shown that the Russian state lacks the institutional framework to apply conditionality, provide assistance or facilitate lesson-drawing aimed at countervailing convergence with EU rules in trade-related policy sectors.[50] At the same time passive leverage through Russian government policies or the Russian market may create an incentive structure for Ukrainian actors to oppose or support convergence with EU rules.[51] Considering Ukraine's strategic importance for Russian government policies in its 'near abroad', we can expect similar complexity in other Eastern neighbourhood countries. The analysis of Ukrainian food safety suggests that high economic dependence on the Russian dairy market decreased the incentives of foreign and domestic dairy producers operating in Ukraine to apply European food safety standards for a long time. Facing a strongly protected and self-sufficient EU market, the Russian market was (and again is) an important alternative export destination for Ukrainian dairy products. The presence of the Russian market does not, however, always create an incentive structure that undermines convergence with EU rules in Ukraine. When Russian government authorities imposed an import ban on Ukrainian dairy products accusing producers of non-compliance with Russian food safety standards, their decision indirectly increased the incentives of Ukraine's dairy producers to take on EU food standards as a means to get access to alternative markets such as the EU single market.

[48]Gawrich *et al.*, (2010); but see Ademmer and Börzel, in this collection.
[49]See also Ademmer and Börzel, in this collection.
[50]See also Dimitrova and Dragneva (2009).
[51]See also Ademmer and Börzel, in this collection.

Russian multinationals play an equally ambivalent role in Ukraine. Contrary to the energy sector, where investments by state-owned Russian energy companies are considered to be an extension of Russian power politics in the Eastern neighbourhood countries, private Russian multinationals investing in Ukraine's telecommunications or dairy sector follow market motivations which are not linked to political motivations.[52] In some policy sectors Russian multinationals exercise active leverage on policy change in Ukraine, thereby contributing to convergence with EU rules. The case of Ukrainian telecommunications suggests that Russian multinationals empower domestic reformers by providing assistance or facilitating lesson-drawing through regulatory networks if the adoption and application of EU rules increases their competitiveness *vis-à-vis* rent-seeking Ukrainian state regulators or firms. In turn, Russian investors in Ukraine's dairy sector lacked such incentives and continued to apply old Soviet standards since they mainly sold their products in Ukraine or exported to the Russian market. Again, we can expect Russian multinationals investing in trade-related sectors in other Eastern neighbourhood countries to have an equally differentiated impact on domestic policy change. If Russian multinationals investing in Ukraine exercise active leverage to promote convergence with EU rules in trade-related fields, similar behaviour of Russian multinationals can be expected in other Eastern neighbourhood countries considering Ukraine's aforementioned high strategic importance for Russia's foreign policy towards its 'near abroad'.

Second, the study provides important insights about the EU's impact on policy change in Ukraine. My findings imply that the EU is not always the key player when it comes to fostering convergence with EU rules in one of its most active and important Eastern neighbours. Thus, similar results can be expected in other Eastern neighbourhood countries. We observe partial convergence with EU rules in the field of telecommunications as early as 2003 despite the absence of EU active leverage to increase domestic incentives and capacities for convergence with EU telecommunications regulations. Further, the EU exercises leverage on policy change in the Eastern neighbourhood countries, which does not, however, always contribute to convergence with EU rules. In the case of Ukrainian dairy, the strongly protected and highly sufficient European dairy market even created an incentive structure that decreased producers' incentives to take on European food safety regulations. Thus, the EU's passive leverage undermined policy change in the Ukrainian dairy sector.

Instead, Western European multinationals operating in Ukraine exercise active leverage on policy change by promoting convergence with EU rules where this is beneficial for them. Like Russian investors, Western European mobile operators had incentives to promote the establishment of an independent regulatory agency that could defend their rights against the dominant state-owned telecoms operator. Hence, they created and empowered a domestic reform coalition by providing assistance to local operators and legislators and by facilitating their participation in regulatory networks. In contrast, Western European investors lacked incentives to employ a similar strategy in Ukraine's dairy sector for the same reasons preventing their Russian counterparts from promoting convergence with EU food safety regulations, i.e. a highly protected and self-sufficient EU dairy market.

My findings suggest that diverse Russian and European forces exercise active and passive leverage on policy change in the Eastern neighbourhood countries. The Russian government

[52]See also Vahtra (2007).

lacks institutional structures to exert active leverage on policy change in trade-related fields. Yet, Russian investments in the Eastern neighbourhood countries, close trade relations with Russia and Russian government policies create opportunity structures for domestic actors that do not necessarily obstruct European integration in the EU's Eastern neighbourhood. Further, my findings show that the EU is, by far, neither the only nor the key external actor that shapes convergence with EU rules. While the Europeanisation scholarship focuses on the EU as the main driver of domestic empowerment, my findings show that non-state actors can apply the same mechanisms as the EU to diversify and empower domestic demand for policy change. Dynamics on the European market as well as Western European multinationals investing in the Eastern neighbourhood countries can actively or passively influence domestic policy choices resulting in increasing convergence with EU rules or inertia. Finally, and in line with the general argument of this collection, this essay has shown that the particular incentives and capacities of key domestic actors needed for convergence explain divergent outcomes. In this respect, multinationals are an understudied external force shaping domestic policy choices in the EU's Eastern neighbourhood.

Freie Universität Berlin

References

Abol'nikov, Y. (1997) 'Na poligone GSM provodyatsya startovye ispytaniya nervov', *Zerkalo Nedeli*, 7, 124, pp. 14–21, February, available at: http://zn.ua/ECONOMICS/na_poligone_gsm_provodyatsya_startovye_ispytaniya_nervov-5893.html, accessed 16 November 2012.

Andonova, L. (2003) *Transnational Politics of the Environment: The EU and Environmental Policy in Central and Eastern Europe* (Cambridge, MA, MIT Press).

Aslund, A. & McFaul, M. (2006) *Revolution in Orange: The Origins of Ukraine's Democratic Breakthrough* (Washington, Carnegie Endowment for International Peace).

Bezborodov, Y. (2001) 'Pravila dlya vsekh—u bol'shikh, u malen'kikh', *Zerkalo Nedeli*, 19, 343, pp. 18–25, May, available at: http://zn.ua/ECONOMICS/pravila_dlya_vseh__i_bolshih,_i_malenkih-24541.html, accessed 16 November 2012.

Blyakha, N. (2009) *Russian Foreign Direct Investment in Ukraine* Electronic Publications of Pan-European Institute 7 (Turku, Turku School of Economics).

Börzel, T. A. (2010) *The Transformative Power of Europe Reloaded. The Limits of External Europeanization*, KFG Working Paper 11 (Berlin, Kolleg-Forschergruppe 'The Transformative Power of Europe', Freie Universität Berlin).

Börzel, T. A. & Pamuk, Y. (2012) 'Pathologies of Europeanization. Fighting Corruption in the Southern Caucasus', *West European Politics*, 35, 1.

Dimitrova, A. & Dragneva, R. (2009) 'Constraining External Governance: Interdependence with Russia and the CIS as Limits to the EU's Rule Transfer in the Ukraine', *Journal of European Public Policy*, 16, 6.

Dries, L. & Swinnen, J. F. M. (2004) 'Foreign Direct Investment, Vertical Integration, and Local Suppliers: Evidence from the Polish Dairy Sector', *World Development*, 32, 9.

EESC (2010) *Opinion of the European Economic and Social Committee on the Future Strategy for the EU Dairy Industry for the Period 2010–2015 and Beyond* (Brussels, European Economic and Social Committee).

Emerson, M., Huw Edwards, T., Gazizullin, I., Lücke, M., Müller-Jentsch, D., Nanivska, V., Pyanitsky, V., Schneider, A., Schweickert, R., Shevtsov, O. & Shumylo, O. (2006) *The Prospects of Deep Free Trade between the European Union and Ukraine* (Brussels, Centre for European Policy Studies).

European Commission (2002a) *Commission Decision of 29 July 2002 Establishing the European Regulators Group for Electronic Communications Networks and Services* 2002/627/EC (Brussels, European Commission).

European Commission (2002b) *Regulation (EC) No 178/2002 of the European Parliament and of the Council of 28 January 2002 Laying Down the General Principles and Requirements of Food Law, Establishing the European Food Safety Authority and Laying Down Procedures in Matters of Food Safety* (Brussels, European Commission).

European Commission (2004a) *European Neighbourhood Policy Strategy Paper* COM (2004) 373 (Brussels, European Commission).

European Commission (2004b) *Regulation (EC) No 852/2004 of the European Parliament and of the Council of 29 April 2004 on the Hygiene of Foodstuffs* (Brussels, European Commission).

European Commission (2005) *The EU–Ukraine Action Plan, 21 February 2005* (Brussels, European Commission).

European Commission (2006) *Progress Report Ukraine, Commission Staff Working Document, Accompanying the Communication from the Commission to the Council and the European Parliament on Strengthening the European Neighbourhood Policy* (Brussels, European Commission).

European Commission (2008) *Communication from the Commission to the European Parliament and the Council, Eastern Partnership* COM (2008) 823 final (Brussels, European Commission).

European Commission (2009) *Progress Report Ukraine, Commission Staff Working Document, Accompanying the Communication from the Commission to the Council and the European Parliament 'Implementation of the European Neighbourhood Policy in 2008'* (Brussels, European Commission).

European Commission & High Representative of the Union for Foreign Affairs and Security Policy (2011) *Implementation of the European Neighbourhood Policy in 2010. Country Report on: Ukraine*, Joint Staff Working Paper (Brussels, European Commission/High Representative of the Union for Foreign Affairs and Security Policy).

European Communities (1997) 'Directive 97/51/EC of the European Parliament and of the Council of 6 October 1997 amending Council Directives 90/387/EEC and 92/44/EEC for the Purpose of Adaptation to a Competitive Environment in Telecommunications', *Official Journal* (OJ L 295), 29 October, available at: http://eur-lex.europa.eu/JOHtml.do?uri=OJ:L:1997:295:SOM:EN:HTML, accessed 16 November 2012.

European Council (1993) *Council Directive 93/43/EEC of 14 June 1993 on the Hygiene of Foodstuffs* (Brussels, European Council).

Filippov, S. (2010) 'Russian Companies: The Rise of New Multinationals', *International Journal of Emerging Markets*, 5, pp. 3–4.

Fischer, S. (2007) 'Die russische Politik gegenüber der Ukraine und Weissrussland', *Aus Politik und Zeitgeschichte*, pp. 8–9.

Freyburg, T., Lavenex, S., Schimmelfennig, F., Skripka, T. & Wetzel, A. (2009) 'EU Promotion of Democratic Governance in the Neighbourhood', *Journal of European Public Policy*, 16, 6.

Galkovskaya, T. (2002) 'Artpodgotovka v VR sostoyalos' obsuzhdenie proektov zakona ukrainy "O Telekommunikatsiyakh". Poka na kruglom stole', *Zerkalo Nedeli*, 44, 419, pp. 15–22, November, available at: http://zn.ua/ECONOMICS/artpodgotovka_v_vr_sostoyalos_obsuzhdenie_proektov_zakona_ukrainy_o_telekommunikatsiyah_poka_na_krug-30221.html, accessed 16 November 2012.

Garcia, M. (2006) *The Challenge of Conforming to Sanitary and Phytosanitary Measures for WTO Accession and EU Exports: The Case of Ukraine* (Rome, Food and Agriculture Organisation of the United Nations).

Gawrich, A., Melnykovska, I. & Schweickert, R. (2010) 'Neighbourhood Europeanization through ENP: The Case of Ukraine', *Journal of Common Market Studies*, 48, 5.

Giorgi, L. & Lindner Friis, L. (2009) 'The Contemporary Governance of Food Safety: Taking Stock and Looking Ahead', *Quality Assurance and Safety of Crops & Foods*, 1, 1.

Gosudarskaya, I. (2009) 'Sovladelets "Terra-Fud": Zhdat' pomoshchi ot gosudarstva bezmyslenno', *Investgazeta*, 38, 19 July.

Gromadzki, G., Sushko, O., Vahl, M., Wolczuk, K. & Wolczuk, R. (2004) *Ukraine and the EU after the Orange Revolution* CEPS Policy Brief 60 (Brussels, Centre for European Policy Studies).

Haughton, T. (2007) 'When Does the EU Make a Difference? Conditionality and the Accession Process in Central and Eastern Europe', *Political Studies Review*, 5, 2.

Haukkala, H. (2009) *From Zero-Sum to Win–Win? The Russian Challenge to the EU's Eastern Neighbourhood Policies* European Policy Analysis 12 (Stockholm, Swedish Institute for European Policy Studies).

Hess, S., Voget, B. & Ryzhkova, M. (2008) *The EU Dairy Market—Real Opportunities for Ukraine?* (Kyiv, Institute for Economic Research and Policy Consulting).

IFC (2009) *Reforming Food Safety Regulations in Ukraine: Proposal for Policymakers* (Kyiv, International Finance Corporation).

Ilgas, S. (2002) '"Telekom" v zakone', *Zerkalo Nedeli*, 43, 418, pp. 9–15, November.

Kornienko, D. (2009) 'Kto na chto uchil'sya. Mobil'nye operatory boryutsya za rynok shirokopolosnogo dostupa', *Zerkalo Nedeli*, 36, 764, 26 September–2 October, available at: http://zn.ua/ECONOMICS/kto_na_chto_uchilsya__mobilnye_operatory_boryutsya_za_rynok_shirokopolosnogo_dostupa-57976.html, accessed 16 November 2012.

Kuksa, V. (2003) 'Pitfalls of the Telecommunications Law', *Zerkalo Nedeli*, 29, 454, pp. 2–8, August.

Kuksa, V. (2006) 'Napugat' ezhika … Ne proshlo i polgoda s momenta zapreta Rossii na vvoz ukrainskogo myasa, Kak Ukraine prigrozila ei tem zhe', *Zerkalo Nedelo*, 13, 592, pp. 8–14, April.

Langbein, J. (2010) *Patterns of Transnationalization and Regulatory Change beyond the EU. Explaining Cross-Sectoral Variation in Ukraine*, unpublished PhD thesis (Florence, European University Institute).

Langbein, J. (2011) *Organizing Regulatory Convergence Outside the EU. Setting Policy-Specific Conditionality and Building Domestic Capacities*, KFG Working Paper 33 (Berlin, Kolleg-Forschergruppe 'The Transformative Power of Europe', Freie Universität Berlin).

Langbein, J. & Wolczuk, K. (2012) 'Convergence without Membership? EU's Impact in the Eastern Neighbourhood: Evidence from Ukraine', *Journal for European Public Policy*, 19, 6.

Larrabee, F. (2010) 'Rethinking Russia: Russia, Ukraine, and Central Europe: The Return of Geopolitics', *Journal of International Affairs*, 63, 2, Spring/Summer.

Lavenex, S. (2008) 'A Governance Perspective on the European Neighbourhood Policy: Integration beyond Conditionality?', *Journal of European Public Policy*, 15, 6.

Lavenex, S. & Schimmelfennig, F. (2009) 'EU Rules beyond EU Borders: Theorizing External Governance in European Politics', *Journal of European Public Policy*, 16, 6.

Levi-Faur, D. (2010) *Regulatory Networks and Regulatory Agencificaton: Toward a Single European Regulatory Space*, Jerusalem Papers in Regulation and Governance, Working Paper 30 (Jerusalem, Hebrew University).

Levitsky, S. & Way, L. (2005) *Linkage versus Leverage: Rethinking the International Dimension of Regime Change* (Syracuse, Campbell Public Affairs Institute, Sawyer Law and Politics Program).

Libman, A. M. & Kheifets, B. A. (2006) *Ekspansiya rossiiskogo kapitala v strany* CNG (Moscow, Ekonomika).

Lieven, A. (2004) 'Europe has Both Moral and Strategic Reasons to Reach Out to Ukraine', *The Times*, 28 December.

Lisitsyn, N., Sutyrin, S., Trofimenko, O. & Vorobieva, I. (2005) 'Russian Telecommunication Company MTS Goes to the CIS', *Journal of East–West Business*, 11, 3/4.

Moody, R. & Polivodsky, O. (2004) *SPS Legislative Gap Analysis—Planning Tool for Future Legal Component Project Interventions. Component of the European Union's TACIS Program for Ukraine Project EuropeAid/114025 C/SV/UA* (Brussels, European Commission).

Nivievskyi, O. & von Cramon-Taubadel, S. (2008) *The Determinants of Dairy Farming Competitiveness in Ukraine*, IER Policy Paper Series AgPP 23 (Kyiv, Institute for Economic Research).

Olearchuk, R. (2011) 'EPIC to Acquire 93% of Ukrtelecom for $1.3bn', *Financial Times*, 13 February.

Oliyarnyk, M. (2005) 'Glavnoe "Ukrtelekom" nakachal telefonnoe pravo', *Kommersant Ukraina*, 2 December, available at: kommersant.ua/doc/631942, accessed 16 November 2012.

Panibratov, A. (2010) *Russian Multinationals: Entry Strategies and Post-entry Operations*, Electronic Publications of Pan-European Institute 15 (Turku, Turku School of Economics and Business Administration).

Pazyuk, A. (2006) *Ukraine. Final Report for the European Commission: Monitoring of Russia and Ukraine (Priority 1) and Armenia, Azerbaijan, Belarus, Georgia, Kazakhstan and Moldova (Priority 2): Telecommunications and the Information Society* (London, Political Intelligence).

PCA (1998) 'Partnership and Co-operation Agreement (PCA) between the European Communities and their member states, and Ukraine, signed on 24/6/1994', *Official Journal* (OJ L 49/3), 19 February.

Popescu, N. & Wilson, A. (2009) *The Limits of Enlargement-Lite: European and Russian Power in the Troubled Neighbourhood* (London, European Council on Foreign Relation).

Primachenko, A. (2002) 'Malen'koe delo sud'i Vasilenko', *Zerkalo Nedeli*, 40, 415, pp. 18–25, October, available at: http://zn.ua/LAW/malenkoe_delo_sudi_vasilenko-29951.html, accessed 16 November 2012.

Reardon, T. & Berdegué, J. (2002) 'The Rapid Rise of Supermarkets in Latin America: Challenges and Opportunities for Development', *Development Policy Review*, 20, 4.

Rose, R. (1991) 'What is Lesson-drawing?', *Journal of Public Policy*, 11, 1.

Schimmelfennig, F. & Sedelmeier, U. (2005) *The Europeanization of Central and Eastern Europe* (Ithaca, NY, Cornell University Press).

Shamota, M. (2011) 'Ukrtelecom's New Owner: "We are not Fronting Akhmetov, the Russians or the Turks"', *Kyivpost*, 23 June.

Shapovalova, N. (2006) *The Russian Federation's Penetration Strategy towards Ukraine* (Toronto, Center for European, Russian, and Eurasian Studies, University of Toronto).

Skibinskaya, M. (2005) '"Kyivstar" bez Kuchmy: istoriya lyubvi i predatel'stva. Chei ty teper'?', *Podrobnosti*, 29 March.

Slaughter, A.-M. (2004) *A New World Order* (Princeton, NJ, Princeton University Press).

Stepanchikov, S. (2007) 'Sud obyazal NKRC vydat' "Kyivstaru" litsenziyu na 3G. Kommissiya—protiv', *Zerkalo Nedeli*, 48, 677, pp. 13–21, December, available at: http://zn.ua/ECONOMICS/sud_obyazal_nkrs_vydat_kievstaru_litsenziyu_na_3g_komissiya__protiv-52178.html, accessed 16 November 2012.

Strubenhoff, H., Kresse, S. & Wilhelm, F. (2007) *Der Ukrainische Milchsektor: Hinweise für potentielle Investoren*, unpublished paper, Kyiv.

Sushko, O. (2008) *The Impact of Russia on Governance Structures in Ukraine*, Discussion Paper 24 (Bonn, Deutsches Institut für Entwicklungspolitik).

Thatcher, M. (2004) 'Winners and Losers in Europeanisation: Reforming the National Regulation of Telecommunications', *West European Politics*, 27, 2.

Vachudova, M. (2005) *Europe Undivided: Democracy, Leverage, and Integration after Communism* (Oxford, Oxford University Press).

Vahtra, P. (2005) *Russian Investments in the CIS; Scope, Motivations and Leverage*, Electronic Publications of Pan-European Institute 9 (Turku, Turku School of Economics and Business Administration).

Vahtra, P. (2007) *Expansion or Exodus?—The New Leaders among the Russian TNCs*, Electronic Publications of Pan-European Institute 13 (Turku, Turku School of Economics and Business Administration).

Vyse, L. (2006) 'Russian Import Ban Hits Ukraine Dairy Industry', *Food Production Daily*, 25 January, available at: http://www.foodproductiondaily.com/Quality-Safety/Russian-import-ban-hits-Ukraine-dairy-industry, accessed 10 September 2008.

Weber, K., Smith, M. E. & Baun, M. (eds) (2007) *Governing Europe's New Neighborhood: Partners or Periphery?* (Manchester, Manchester University Press).

Wendler, F. (2008) 'The Public–Private Regulation of Food Safety through HACCP: What Does it Mean for the Governance Capacity of Public and Private Actors?', in Vos, E. (ed.) (2008) *European Risk Governance: Its Science, its Inclusiveness and its Effectiveness* (Mannheim, Mannheim University Press).

Wolczuk, K. (2008) *Adjectival Europeanisation? The Impact of the European Neighbourhood Policy on Ukraine*, Global Europe Papers 11 (Bath & Nottingham, University of Bath & University of Nottingham).

World Bank (2004) *Ukraine Trade Policy Study (In Two Volumes), Volume II: Main Report, Poverty Reduction and Economic Management Unit Europe and Central Asia Region* (Washington, DC, World Bank).

World Bank (2005) *Electronic Communications in Ukraine: The Bottleneck to Sustainable Development* (Washington, DC, World Bank).

World Bank (2007) *Food Safety and Agricultural Health Management in CIS Countries: Completing the Transition* (Washington, DC, World Bank).

Yakovlev, A. (2006) 'The Evolution of Business–State Interaction in Russia: From State Capture to Business Capture?', *Europe-Asia Studies*, 58, 7.

Yarovaya, L. (2003) 'Mobil'nye operatory srazhayutsya za chastoty', *Zerkalo Nedeli*, 8, 433, pp. 1–7, March.

Shaping Convergence with the EU in Foreign Policy and State Aid in Post-Orange Ukraine: Weak External Incentives, Powerful Veto Players

ANTOANETA DIMITROVA & RILKA DRAGNEVA

Abstract

This essay analyses convergence with EU rules in Ukraine in two policy areas—foreign and security policy and state aid regulation. Comparing the two, we find different levels of convergence, somewhat higher in foreign policy (but slowing down after 2010) than in state aid law regulation. We explain this by analysing the presence and actions of oligarchs as veto players that have had an extensive influence on policy in the Ukrainian political system in recent years. In policy areas where convergence with EU rules negatively affects the interests of oligarchs and their political allies, we see only limited convergence with EU legislation and policies.

DEBATES ABOUT THE INFLUENCE OF THE EUROPEAN UNION (EU) on its Eastern neighbours have gone from post-enlargement optimism to tempered realism. Based on the literature that has studied the effects of enlargement, the optimistic notes in this debate came from the understanding that the EU has, by and large, succeeded in transferring its norms and rules to candidate states from the East and contributed to their democratic and market transformations. The pessimism came as observers took note of the EU's enlargement fatigue and the diminished power of conditionality when membership was not a realistic prospect. The European Neighbourhood Policy (ENP) and the Eastern Partnership (EP) initiative were both instruments created in the aftermath of the EU's eastern enlargement to deal with aspiring members such as Ukraine and Moldova and to facilitate their transformations to democracy and the market economy. The ENP in particular drew on the experiences and expertise gathered by the Commission during the last enlargement in terms of both personnel and policy tools (Kelley 2006). However, it soon became clear that in the case of the EU's Eastern partners and especially potential candidates such as Ukraine and Moldova, the ENP was seen as both insufficient (from the perspective of aspirant members) and ineffective (from the EU perspective) in promoting further reform in the way enlargement conditionality had done. The weakening influence of the EU on Ukraine and other neighbourhood states begs the question of whether the EU has lost its ability to inspire and guide reform in neighbouring states or even whether the Union's transformative power was only ever effective in combination with pro-European preferences of domestic actors, as it was in Central and Eastern Europe.

The EU's ENP partners are expected to converge with EU rules in a number of areas defined by the ENP's Action Plan, the EU's Progress Reports and partnership agreements between the EU and the ENP states.[1] This essay aims to examine the extent of convergence with EU rules, defined as policy change, either change of sector-specific legislation or rhetorical commitment to such a change, or ultimately, behavioural compliance with EU policies that do not fit domestic policy. The question of how the EU can stimulate convergence with its rules on markets, energy, foreign policy or other key areas in its neighbourhood can be answered better if we have a deeper understanding of the mechanisms that have influenced convergence so far. To determine convergence or the lack thereof, we examine the formal adoption or amendment of legislation, rhetorical commitments, especially in Common Foreign and Security Policy (CFSP), and behavioural change where evidence for such change is available with a clear indication that it is linked to EU policies.

We examine convergence in two different kinds of policy areas—namely, foreign policy and state aid regulation, the latter being part of the core of the internal market *acquis*. We argue that domestic factors and, more specifically, the positions of key veto players, can best explain a differential pattern of convergence where Ukraine makes policy changes in response to some of the EU's policy-specific requirements but ignores or resists others. To develop our argument, we focus on key formal and informal veto players and their role in shaping reforms or maintaining the *status quo* in an internal market-related area and in foreign policy.

The choice of these policy fields is led by the key question informing this collection, namely, why does policy change under EU guidance vary between policy fields. Furthermore, our two cases display different levels of institutionalisation of the EU *acquis*: CFSP and European Security and Defence Policy (ESDP) is an area with very few EU rules, and it can therefore be defined as weakly institutionalised, while state aid law is part of a core *acquis* area which has complex substantive and procedural rules. State aid has been an area of high delegation to the European Commission, which has sought to establish a technocratic approach to monitoring and controlling the provision of aid, and has the potential for hierarchical rule transfer in relation to substantive rules.

Building on arguments that stress the fact that the EU's credibility in enlargement has decreased due to both enlargement fatigue and the reluctance to offer Ukraine the prospect of accession, we find it important to offer a domestic perspective on convergence and examine the changed configuration of veto players and their preferences.

Recent analyses of Ukraine have been conducted in the context of a pro-Western configuration of veto players—the period of government of President Viktor Yushchenko after the Orange Revolution. In 2010, this came to an end with the inauguration of President Viktor Yanukovich. Throughout 2010 and 2011, Yanukovich made gradual but continuous changes, consolidating his hold on power and reversing the freedoms that gave Ukraine its democratic credentials. These dramatic changes require a new analysis of Ukraine's convergence with the EU that takes into account the role of a different set of domestic veto

---

[1]We would like to thank one of the anonymous reviewers for this point.

players and the incentives offered by external actors (the EU but also sometimes others such as World Trade Organization, WTO).

More specifically, we argue that the presidential election of 2010 led to further enhancement of the power of oligarchs, especially those linked to the Party of Regions (*Partiya Regionov*) and to even less interest in convergence with EU rules. The general context of recent deterioration of democratic institutions and increased pro-Russian orientation makes a re-examination of the case of Ukraine and its convergence with EU rules especially interesting.

Before we proceed to investigate how specific policy areas have fared, in the next section we briefly address some influential theoretical approaches that have informed debates in this area.

Theoretical approaches to the explanation of convergence

The conceptualisation of the EU's influence on its neighbours, especially the states situated in South and Eastern Europe, has been strongly influenced by the literature on EU enlargement and its findings. The main conclusion from this literature, namely that the EU has been quite influential in supporting democratic consolidation and market reforms in post-communist states which have been involved in accession negotiations, has also now been taken on board by policy makers, to the extent that the EU started advertising enlargement as its most successful foreign policy tool (Rehn 2007). This literature also identified the most effective EU policy tool: conditionality and the mechanism behind it, namely external incentives and threats affecting domestic actors. The problem with enlargement-based policy tools and underlying mechanisms after the 2004–2007 enlargement of the EU is, simply, that the EU cannot continuously enlarge in order to influence its neighbours. Even before the accession of Bulgaria and Romania in 2007, there was a feeling that the EU and its older member states in particular were suffering from enlargement fatigue and would not engage in further expansion in the near future (Rehn 2006).

Analysis of the situation of Ukraine following the external incentives model (Schimmelfennig & Sedelmeier 2005; Vachudova 2005) would examine whether domestic actors adopt EU rules (leading to policy convergence in specific sectors) based on the ratio between the costs of compliance and the benefits from EU rewards. The problem with this, however, is that, in the ENP context, the benefits that the EU has been able to offer do not include membership. In our view, the membership perspective adds a critical edge to EU incentives which are not only material but contain an element of symbolism and identity (Dimitrova 2004; Steunenberg & Dimitrova 2007). Furthermore, the credibility of EU conditions is much diminished without an officially recognised candidate status.

Bearing these considerations in mind, the EU has tried to develop an incentive which replaces enlargement and which is sufficiently interesting for Ukraine (and other EP countries) to keep reforming and complying with its demands for change. Having refrained from giving an explicit membership perspective, the EU offered Ukraine a stake in its internal market instead (European Commission 2004, p. 3) or the possibility to create a Deep and Comprehensive Free Trade Area (DCFTA) between the EU and Ukraine as well as some sector-specific incentives. Thus any potentially effective EU conditionality must be seen in the context of the rewards offered by the DCFTA, the Association Agreement and the potential economic benefits from it. Provisions for regulatory convergence in the Partnership and Cooperation Agreement (PCA) and in the future Association Agreement embody the EU approach of promoting its *acquis*-based regulatory framework as a model for third states. These agreements serve, to a great extent, to encourage third countries in their regulatory frameworks to converge towards the *acquis* of the Union as a way to reap the benefits of trade.

There are several authors who argue that, at the aggregate level, the incentives offered by the EU in the context of the ENP and the DCFTA are not strong enough to compensate for the possible losses of domestic actors that may result from adaptation to EU requirements (Melnykovska & Schweickert 2008, p. 446; Valasek 2010; Lange 2010). To evaluate convergence with the EU, we try to identify the actors which may be relevant as veto players able to stop changes in a particular sector. Before we do this, we put forward one general argument, namely that *a priori* the EU has less leverage in Ukraine than it did in Central and Eastern Europe. We will explain briefly why we consider this to be the case.

We find that the external incentives model and related explanations highlighting the EU's conditionality approach were the best explanatory frameworks for the success of Central and Eastern European states in EU rule adoption in the last enlargement. We believe, however, that some of the scope conditions necessary for the mechanisms described in this model to work are not present in Ukraine as they were in Central and Eastern Europe. On the EU supply side, EU conditionality was generally credible in the case of candidate states included in the Eastern enlargement. In the case of Ukraine, not only has the EU balked at ever giving a clear enlargement perspective, but the Union's general state of constitutional crisis in the post-Lisbon treaty era makes this unlikely to happen in the near future. As specified in the external incentives framework, when EU credibility is low, the likelihood of adoption of its rules is lower (Schimmelfennig 2001).

Why is the prospect of joining the EU so important? After all, the EU has adjusted its policies and offers incentives such as the DCFTA that may be sufficient for domestic actors that stand to benefit from the opening of trade. Still, we believe that next to the anticipated material benefits, the symbolic award of joining the EU was an essential component of the incentives offered by the EU in the last enlargement process and this is also the case for Ukraine. In the last enlargement, Central European leaders used a strategy of rhetorical entrapment, arguing that accession to the EU would be a return to the European community of democratic states for their countries. For EU leaders to refuse to accept them would be equal to challenging their own commitment to democracy (Schimmelfennig 2000), but the use of rhetoric applied in both directions—governments from Bulgaria to Poland had promised their electorates that they would lead their countries into the EU. The symbolic reward mattered to them and kept them on track even when specific sectoral costs of adjustment were high (Dimitrova 2004; Fink Hafner 1999; Henderson 1999).[2] Symbolism is also important in the case of Ukraine—for example, symbolic recognition of Ukraine's importance to the EU or European identity. The EU has, however, underestimated the symbolic aspects of its relationship with Ukraine (Popescu & Wilson 2009).

Not only is the EU failing to emphasise the symbolic aspects of its relations with Ukraine,[3] but in Ukraine itself discourses of the 'return to Europe' are not very prominent

---

[2]As Fink Hafner (1999, p. 789) has noted, the symbolism of a successful 'return to Europe' or of joining the EU became an autonomous force for legitimising post-communist political elites in Central and Eastern Europe.

[3]Most recent evidence of this is provided by the attendance at the Eastern Partnership Summit in Warsaw in September 2011. Analysts have commented on the lower level representation by France and the UK (Rettman 2011).

(Popescu & Wilson 2009, p. 16). These differences lead us to suggest that, on the whole, the EU's incentives for domestic actors in Ukraine are much weaker across the board than they were in the last enlargement, even if there are specific sectoral gains to be made.

Another possibility is that the EU may be able to promote its rules in different sectors through networks as described by the so-called external governance approach. The key argument of the external governance literature (Lavenex 2008; Lavenex & Schimmelfennig 2009) is that the EU aims strategically to promote and export its own regulatory regimes to third countries and especially to neighbouring states. Furthermore, this approach suggests that the EU's rule promotion is, in the absence of enlargement incentives, conducted at the sectoral level through the horizontal contacts between actors and networks involved in applying the regulatory frameworks. The ENP is seen, in this context, as an instrument for cooperation in areas where the EU and its partners are looking for joint problem solving and where they establish cooperation in the economic sphere accompanied by horizontal ties between the public administrations of neighbouring countries and the EU.

This explanation expects that the EU would be better able to promote rules in areas which are highly institutionalised and enjoy high internal legitimacy in the EU (Lavenex & Schimmelfennig 2009, pp. 802–3). Based on this, we cannot make a clear prediction how partners would deal with the EU's state aid rules, as this is a highly institutionalised and still controversial area in which member states have not always complied with common rules.

More importantly, we find it misleading to focus on the EU's ability to promote convergence through technical or horizontal or network channels when the 'recipient' is a state with strong hierarchical organisation such as Ukraine. Analysts (Lange 2010; Valasek 2010; Wilson 2010, 2011) agree that the actions of President Yanukovich since he came to power have aimed at strengthening the vertical separation of power and diminishing the role of institutions such as the judiciary. Key administrative posts are often taken by business representatives or their supporters. We find that the context of a centralised administrative state is not conducive to forming effective horizontal networks that may promote convergence with the EU.

The centralising tendency visible in post-Orange Ukraine leads us to believe that we should look at key domestic veto players rather than transnational networks to explain the dynamics of convergence. Before proceeding to this analysis, we need to briefly consider how to conceptualise the role of Russia as an important regional player.

Dimitrova and Dragneva (2009) have argued that the effects of EU governance cannot be examined in a vacuum and need to be considered against the influence of Russia as a powerful regional hegemon. They have shown that interdependence with Russia is a significant factor when considering Ukraine's convergence with EU rules. They have also suggested that interdependencies with Russia differ in different policy areas: from high in energy and foreign policy to diminishing in trade. Based on this perspective, we can expect that Ukraine will take into account regional context and important geopolitical factors, among them Russia's very presence and power when aligning its foreign policy with the EU.[4]

[4]We use alignment with EU foreign policy as synonymous with convergence, as the Union's foreign policy does not require much regulatory adaptation. By contrast, internal market-related areas, such as state aid or company law, require more serious adaptation with a larger body of EU *acquis*. In those cases it makes sense to look for convergence by means of adopting concrete regulatory measures.

Russia's influence, however, cannot be understood without reference to domestic politics and its key role as the energy supplier for Ukraine's economy, providing gas for the metallurgical industry and other energy intensive sectors. We therefore aim to examine Russia's influence through the prism of domestic actors' preferences and how these may be influenced by Russia's strategy of linking geopolitical choices by its neighbours and the politics of gas.

Focusing on the domestic arena: veto players

By focusing on veto players, we build on two sets of explanations. The first is the above-mentioned external incentives model which placed domestic actors and their cost–benefit calculations at the centre of the explanation. We find, however, as argued above, that the EU's incentives are weak and less credible than they were in the last enlargement. Therefore, along with other existing studies that have explicitly pointed to the role of veto players in Ukraine (Melnykovska & Schweickert 2008), we examine developments in the domestic arena as the decisive factor influencing convergence.[5]

We suggest that reforms in Ukraine can be best analysed as changes in the *status quo* in a specific sector or policy area. As the incentive of enlargement is absent, the EU's influence is one among many that influence the strategic calculations of veto players. Veto players are defined as actors whose agreement is needed to change the *status quo* (Tsebelis 2002, pp. 17–19). Tsebelis, in his seminal work, defines two categories of veto players, namely institutional (for example presidency and parliament) and partisan (political parties and relevant majorities) (2002, p. 19). As he has suggested, analyses of individual veto players can include actors who are crucial for agreement in a specific area even if they are not institutional veto players (2002, p. 81).

As has been argued elsewhere, post-communist systems are characterised by the crucial role played by informal veto players, the so-called early winners of economic reform (Hellman 1998, p. 233). Ganev has shown that these post-communist entrepreneurs have created powerful networks that have captured the state and penetrated its structures (2007). An important consequence of state capture is that business interests play the role of veto players in government and parliament, which includes the possibility of vetoing EU-driven reform as well (Dimitrova 2010). In Ukraine, the influence of oligarchic clans on political power continues beyond the transition to democracy period and is characterised by a strategy for wealth accumulation dubbed 'power = money = power' by Melnykovska and Schweickert (2008). As they explain, access to state power allows oligarchs to secure their economic interests and make profits which they use to broaden their political power (2008, p. 448).

We expect, therefore, that sector-specific convergence effects in Ukraine will depend on the extent to which the policy change advocated by the EU affects the interests of these formal and informal veto players (Melnykovska & Schweickert 2008; Dimitrova 2010; Dragneva & Dimitrova 2010). We will examine how sector-specific configurations of formal and informal veto players and these players' interests may be affected by EU demands for convergence.

[5]See also Buzogány, and Ademmer and Börzel, in this collection.

In the next section we discuss briefly who the relevant actors are and what knowledge we already have of their preferences in EU-related issues such as market reforms or foreign policy.

Who are the important actors?

There is an extensive literature which discusses the nature of Ukraine's political institutions and, more specifically, the extent to which they have been penetrated and captured by oligarchic groups (Darden 2001; Puglisi 2003; Way 2004; D'Anieri 2007; Flikke 2008). Oligarchic groups and oligarchs, such as Firtash and Achmetov, can be considered informal veto players in the sense that they are not always empowered directly by the Ukrainian constitutional and institutional system, but are able to stop any policy change by virtue of their penetration of the state and close links with executive and parliamentary actors.

To understand this, we need to take into account that Ukrainian transition has resulted in the establishment of a stable system of rent-seeking and rent-giving between president, parliament (*Rada*), government and big business. The more important an institution has been, the more it has been targeted by non-state actors. The presidency has, throughout the 1990s, established itself as the institutional basis for the formation of a neo-patrimonial regime built on regional clan networks (Puglisi 2003; Way 2004). The powers of the president were somewhat limited by the *Rada* with the constitutional changes negotiated in December 2004, yet President Yushchenko did not break from this system, proceeding to promote his 'Orange' business supporters (Wilson 2009; Malygina 2010).

The *Rada* was also an important source of influence and indeed became a key target for big business to the extent that promulgation of legislation in the 1998 and 2002 parliaments became critically dependent on the fluid support of a number of loosely organised factions (Puglisi 2003). While big business was behind all political factions, the backers of the Party of Regions became key players during the 2006 and 2007 parliaments. This was due to the electoral success of the Party of Regions, but also because changes in the constitutional set-up led to a smaller number of factions in the *Rada*, hence a simpler bargaining process in law and policy making. Despite their critical role in the *Rada*, the Party of Regions and its parliamentary allies, the Communist Party (*Komunistichna Partiya*) and the Socialist Party (*Sotsialistichna Partiya*), were frequently locked in conflicts with the presidency during the Yushchenko period, which resulted in extensive constitutional and political battles (Wilson 2009).

The election of President Yanukovich in 2010 changed the political landscape in several important ways. It meant that the presidency was back in the hands of the Party of Regions, which also had a healthy parliamentary majority. Thus, the big businesses behind the governing party gained a firmer grasp on the political system. Further, reminiscent of the Kuchma presidency, we see the renewed importance of the president as an arbiter dividing and ruling between the different groupings within the Party of Regions. The political and constitutional changes initiated by Yanukovich have led to the reconcentration of power into the hands of the presidency. We see a closer similarity to a neo-patrimonial regime than in the preceding period (Malygina 2010).

Inside the Party of Regions, two different informal factions emerged as veto players. The first group was the faction around the Donetsk-based oligarch Rinat Achmetov, and the second, described as more a conservative and pro-Russian group, was formed around those linked to energy companies such as Dmitry Firtash, former boss of RosUkrEnergo, and the Minister of Energy Yurii Boiko. The most important feature of this second group of informal veto players, the so-called 'gas lobby', is that they are closely connected to companies that thrive on 'market distortion, government manipulation, monopolies and administrative resources' (Lange 2010, p. 4). Furthermore, and crucially important for our analysis, Firtash has reportedly been the biggest financial backer of Yanukovich's electoral campaign (Wilson 2009; Marone 2010).

Preferences of key veto players

The formal, institutional veto players in the Ukrainian system are the parliament and especially the president. Due to his constitutional role in foreign policy, the president's preferences are central in foreign-policy decisions. Here it is useful to remember that President Yanukovich himself owed his electoral support to the Russian-speaking eastern part of Ukraine. In this sense, convergence with Russia may be expected to be one of the main factors ensuring continuous support from his electorate (White & McAllister 2009, pp. 231–32).

Next to the presidency, another set of key veto players are the partisan veto players with a majority in the *Rada*, currently the Party of Regions (*Partiya Regioniv*). This group, however, is not homogeneous. As the discussion in the previous paragraphs shows, within the Party of Regions different oligarchic factions play an independent role. They may pursue different interests and the president can act as an arbiter, balancing between them or deciding which one would dominate political and business life.

As for the informal actors, adding to the discussion in the previous sections we can expect, following Moravcsik (1998, pp. 38–41), that the structure of the economy and the importance of key sectors would lead to the aggregation of preferences of certain business and sector interests into the preferences of the government. The fact that Ukraine has been a weak or captured state means, however, that the domestic preferences which are aggregated at the government level would be mostly the preferences of oligarchs, defined by the key industries and assets that they own. A further complication is added by the efforts of the presidency to balance the interests of oligarchic factions in a process that is neither transparent nor predictable.

Bearing all this in mind, we can rely on empirical sources which have identified the interests of major factions and oligarchs in order to define their preferences. We can assume that oligarchs whose wealth is based on industries that export mostly to Russia, as well as gas oligarchs, will favour policies that will not damage relations with Russia. We also expect that oligarchs and supporting factions will resist regulatory changes that would limit state capture in general. This would be true of oligarchs favoured by the presidency of Yushchenko as well as of those oligarchs linked to Yanukovich and the Party of Regions.

There are some previous analyses supporting our expectations. In terms of substantive preferences, Wolczuk has pointed out that many sectors of the Ukrainian economy are characterised by technological backwardness and lack of competitiveness. This lack of modernisation of industry does not appear to hinder so much economic ties with Russia and the CIS (Wolczuk 2004, p. 7). Smolar similarly suggests that Ukraine's outdated industrial base has maintained its output based on low wages, low prices of energy and state subsidies. Ukrainian elites, according to him, have aimed to avoid the social costs of modernisation and therefore have continued to rely on low-quality exports for the Russian market.

If Ukraine were to give in to EU demands for elimination of state subsidies—as the required legislation in state aid would do—then Ukrainian exports could become too expensive for Russian markets (Smolar 2006).

The same is valid for gas imports. As Ćwiek-Karpowicz (2010, p. 262) has pointed out, the interests of oligarchs who have controlled energy-intensive sectors of Ukrainian industry were threatened by the high price of gas during the Yushchenko years. Their priority, as exemplified by President Yanukovich's pre-election promises, has been an agreement with Russia for cheaper gas imports. Despite some analyses (Melnykovska & Schweickert 2008, p. 454) which have argued that the opportunities for cheaper gas imports have been exhausted, the closing of the so-called gas-for-fleet deal in 2010 showed that both Ukraine and Russia were interested in continuing the symbiosis between energy policy and foreign policy.[6] Furthermore, as Wilson (2010, p. 2) has specified, the business model of Ukrainian oligarchs has relied on gas arbitrage profits. Securing cheap Russian gas appears to be the key preference of gas and energy oligarchs.

Other analyses suggest that oligarchic clans have been changing and that their interests bring them closer to the EU. Melnykovska and Schweickert (2008) have argued that changes in the preferences of oligarchic clans from accumulation towards security and consolidation would become the key bottom-up force for institutional convergence between Ukraine and the EU. They have claimed that these oligarchs can become a force for greater alignment with European and international norms. Their analysis, however, is focused mostly on the oligarchs who supported Yushchenko and the Orange Revolution, and even in their case we believe that lack of convergence in a number of areas such as company law shows that policy-specific veto players and their interests prevail (Dragneva & Dimitrova 2010). Melnykovska and Schweickert cite as evidence the constitutional changes under Yushchenko moving the Ukrainian system towards a parliamentary republic (2008, p. 450). We must note, however, that these changes have been reversed under President Yanukovich and so has much of the progress in good governance which they base their arguments on.[7]

Substantive preferences on specific issues may differ between oligarchs; however, based on previous work we can confidently suggest that the oligarchs' main interests are determined by what maximises the preservation of their own autonomy in economic and political terms, property rights acquired during privatisation and influence upon political life.[8] As a recent policy brief argues (Matuszak 2011), 'the introduction of free and honest competition on the Ukrainian market and the influx of foreign investments would pose a threat to the monopolistic position of oligarchs'.

[6]According to the agreement signed in April 2010 between President Yanukovich and Russia's President Medvedev, Ukraine extended the lease to station the Russian Black Sea Fleet in Sevastopol for the next 25 years in exchange for a 30% discount in the price of Russian gas deliveries (but not more than US$100 per 1,000 m[3]). See Centre for Eastern Studies, available at: http://www.osw.waw.pl/en/publikacje/eastweek/2011-09-07/ukrainianrussian-gas-dispute, accessed 3 October 2011.

[7]According to Freedom House ratings, Ukraine dropped from the free to the partly free category in 2010. In a survey of economic freedom by the Heritage Foundations and the *Wall Street Journal*, Ukraine was rated 164th out of 179 countries in 2010—behind Russia, Belarus and Kazakhstan and in the lowest place among all European countries.

[8]A study of legal reform in the area of company law shows, for example, that oligarchs have aimed primarily at the preservation of privatisation gains and influenced accordingly the voting behaviour of the Party of Regions despite fairly constant external pressure for legislative alignment with EU norms in this field (Dragneva & Dimitrova 2010).

We argue therefore that the most important preference of oligarchs is the preservation of the regulatory and institutional *status quo*. This key assumption is at the core of our policy sector analyses.

In this sense, if EU-related legislation limits oligarchs' autonomy, it would be highly unrealistic to expect that they would allow it to reach the stage of implementation. State aid and other market-regulatory legislation clearly have the potential to limit access to subsidies and freedom of operation and thus would be particularly sensitive to convergence following this logic.

Not only are the preferences of another set of oligarchs represented by this presidency, as compared to the Yushchenko period, but, bearing in mind President Yanukovich's moves to strengthen his own position by balancing between the factions, his role may also become more important. In our view, there is evidence of a complex informal order through which business preferences are balanced at the level of the presidency.[9] This means that when oligarchs do not have strong views on a policy area, the president's preferences will be crucial. This would be, according to us, the case with foreign policy.

Therefore our expectation would be to see diminishing convergence with the EU policies, based on the pro-Russian preferences of President Yanukovich, an important constitutional veto player. We also expect his preferences to converge with the interests of the dominant factions of the Party of Regions, which would be determined by the negative imperative of not angering Russia.

More specifically, the interests of the gas lobby faction within the Party of Regions, given their enrichment through the import of gas, can be assumed to be against foreign policy actions that affect negatively relations with Russia. During Putin's presidency and especially during his term as prime minister, Russia's strategy has been to create issue linkages between gas and foreign policy (Popescu & Wilson 2009, p. 44; Ademmer & Börzel, in this collection). Russia's concerns with relation to Ukraine are often geopolitical and foreign-policy related—such as the issue of the Russian fleet's stay in the Crimea (Ćwiek-Karpowicz 2010, p. 1; Popescu & Wilson 2009, pp. 41–44). Thus the preference of oligarchs linked to President Yanukovich for a gas deal with Russia leads to concessions on foreign-policy issues important to Russia such as NATO aspirations or the Black Sea fleet. As Puglisi has aptly noted, 'as long as Russia views Ukraine as the main battlefield in its zero-sum geostrategic game with the West, Ukrainian business representatives are likely to become Russia's willing instruments in this confrontation' (2008, p. 81).

In the following sections of the essay, we examine the actual convergence in foreign policy on the one hand and state aid on the other, and the role of political actors in this process.

Convergence and divergence in foreign and security policy

To determine whether Ukraine has converged towards EU policies and requirements in the area of foreign policy, we start from the observation that the demands of the EU in this area have not been extensive. While the ENP was partly created to manage relations with

[9]For example, President Yanukovich's December 2010 reorganisation formally cut the number of ministers, but other changes broadened the scope of influence of deputy prime ministers linked to the Donetsk group of oligarchs, balancing their influence with the influence of the gas faction (Centre for Eastern Studies, available at: http://www.osw.waw.pl/en/publikacje/eastweek/2010-12-15/ukraine-s-president-balances-out-groups-influence, accessed 26 September 2011).

neighbours so as to extend stability and security beyond the EU's borders, the Union's aspirations in terms of CFSP are surprisingly modest. This reflects the EU's traditional way of promoting stability through regional integration and trade rather than aiming to form alliances on foreign-policy issues. Furthermore, the EU's role in this part of the world has been subordinated to NATO. When we look at security issues, it has been the dispute over Ukraine's wish to join NATO under President Yushchenko that has overshadowed relations. The EU, true to its soft power *modus operandi*, has expected Eastern members of the ENP to consult and align with CFSP declarations and sanctions open for alignment. The EU's second biggest concern has been border security and containing regional conflicts such as the Transnistrian conflict. The EU has expected Ukraine to 'cooperate constructively with the EU' on all issues related to Transnistria settlement efforts (European Commission 2004, 2006, 2010a). Last but not least, the EU has encouraged the participation of Ukraine in peacekeeping operations in the Balkans and more recently in the EU naval operation Atlanta (European Commission, 2010a, p. 6).

On the whole, we must note that the EU's demands in the area of foreign policy are not high because this policy area is a weak spot for the Union itself. Institutionalisation is weak inside the EU, so while incentives may not be high, it looks as if convergence would not be very costly for Ukraine either. In this case we may expect low convergence based on low levels of policy activity in the EU itself.

The picture, however, becomes more interesting when we take into account rhetoric and symbolic actions and the fact that even symbolic commitments by Ukraine in some areas may matter to Russia as they concern a key state in its neighbourhood. Russia's adamant opposition to Ukraine's NATO entry is the best example of how sensitive it is to challenges in its 'near abroad'. Furthermore, as Popescu and Wilson (2009, p. 30) have argued, Russia has made the idea of Slavic brotherhood with Ukraine and Belarus a cornerstone of its post-Orange Revolution strategy to win influence among its neighbours.[10] In such a context, and given Russia's discourse stressing common Eastern Orthodox Christian roots, Ukrainian actions to support EU sanctions against Belarus may be costly for the president.

Looking at Ukraine's convergence with EU foreign policy in this light we note some variation over time. Progress in aligning Ukrainian policies with the EU up to 2009 is noted in the Report on the Negotiations of the Association Agreement of Ukraine with the EU. The chapters dealing with cooperation and convergence in the field of foreign and security policy have been provisionally closed. According to one Ukrainian official, the least convergence had been achieved in the area of military cooperation:

> Both Brussels and Kyiv failed to adequately assess all the potential difficulties of military cooperation. It took Ukraine too long to develop a comprehensive plan for utilising the hazardous legacy of the Soviet Army. The European Union underestimated the dependency of security and defence measures on the availability of funds. Today the parties understand how they should proceed but we wasted a lot of time. (Veselovsky 2008)

In terms of crisis management and peacekeeping under the EU's ESDP, Ukraine has been praised for taking part in several EU missions. Ukraine's contribution to the EU's

---

[10]Another illustration of how Russia uses the symbolism of fraternity is the presentation of Presidents Yanukovich and Lukashenko with awards for contributing to the cause of Orthodox Christianity in January 2011.

border assistance mission at the Ukrainian–Moldovan border has been praised by the EU. Ukraine has also been seen as a valuable contributor to the EU police mission in Bosnia & Hercegovina and the EU police mission in the Former Yugoslav Republic of Macedonia (named EUPOL Proxima). Furthermore, already under the Yanukovich leadership, in October 2010 Ukraine expressed its intent to join two EU 'battlegroups' (established under ESDP) and made a list of assets that it might incorporate in these (Hale 2010).

In terms of the overall picture in foreign policy however, other analyses suggest domestic capacity for taking a unified stance in foreign policy was limited during the Yushchenko years. The internal strife between the president and the prime minister during that period has been reflected also in different visions on foreign policy. Thus, according to Stegnyi, different political players tried to adjust the foreign policy vision to their own needs and interests, pursuing 'inconsistent and disparate foreign policy priorities' (2011, p. 62). The institutional consolidation of power around the presidency which we have discussed above means that there has been less fragmentation in the formulation of Ukraine's position, although this does not necessarily lead to coherent and one-directional foreign-policy orientation given Ukraine's traditional balancing act (Wilson 2010).

It can be argued, however, that the concentration of power in the presidency together with the dominance of the Party of Regions in the *Rada* allows the president more room for manoeuvre for foreign-policy moves. This is a policy area in which we expected Yanukovich's allegiance to Russia to produce a shift. A clear sign of this shift taking place has been the conclusion of the landmark agreement on Russia's Black Sea fleet (much resisted by pro-Western Ukrainian politicians).

As mentioned above, in April 2010 Presidents Medvedev and Yanukovich signed the gas-for-fleet agreement, prolonging the stay of the Russian Black Sea fleet in Sevastopol for another 25 years after 2017, with the possibility of an extension for another five years (Lange 2010, p. 3). Analysts have commented that this deal shows the lack of effectiveness of EU foreign policy in Ukraine even if it does not affect formal EU demands defined by the Commission.[11] Even if EU demands for formal convergence in the CFSP are minimal and do not include such issues, the deal affects the EU's prospects to develop a strategic role in the region. It also goes against the Union's long-held wish to include the bilateral deal with Russia into a wider strategic framework.[12] It is indicative of the strength of the presidency that this long-term commitment, with serious geopolitical implications, was dealt with only briefly in the Ukrainian parliament. According to Lange, 'the ratification of the Black Sea Fleet deal and the passing of the national budget in the parliament took only eight minutes' (Lange 2010, p. 4).

The other significant development that signalled a change of direction in foreign policy was the formulation of new foreign policy guidelines by the president. President

---

[11] *The Financial Times Brussels Blog* scathingly commented that Commissioner Fule's indifference to this deal during his visit to Ukraine in the same week in which it was signed led to 'surreal consequences'; available at: http://blogs.ft.com/brusselsblog/2010/04/russia-teaches-eu-a-lesson-in-its-ukraine-gas-for-naval-base-deal, accessed 26 April 2011.

[12] Pop (2011) reports a Commission proposal announced in September 2011 to enable the EU to negotiate strategic energy contracts with other countries and have a greater say when other countries strike bilateral deals with Russia.

Yanukovich presented the new set of foreign policy guidelines in March 2010.[13] Introducing the new guidelines, the president suggested that the choice of Ukraine was to aim for 'maximally close collaboration without integration' with the Euro-Atlantic structures.[14] He stressed the non-aligned status of Ukraine and the necessity to maintain it, which would appear to be a change from the firmly pro-EU line of the previous administration and a return to former President Kuchma's so-called 'multi-vector' policy which paid lip service to European integration, but focused on Russia.

A similar interpretation is offered by analysis from the Razumkov Centre, suggesting that the changed foreign policy guidelines must be interpreted as reorienting the country away from the EU and towards Russia, as especially evidenced by the claim that the new security architecture of Europe should be seen to consist not only of EU countries but also of 'neighbours and partners' of the EU such as Ukraine, Russia, Belarus and Moldova.[15] Other analysts such as Wilson (2010) have interpreted Yanukovich's moves in foreign policy as a sequential balancing act.

While we agree with this assessment, it is worth noting that energy security is defined by the president as the most important aspect of security for Ukraine.[16] Given our previous discussion of Russia's use of energy for foreign policy goals, this emphasis on energy security means that if Ukraine were to be faced with a choice between Russia and the EU, Russian interests would prevail.

The energy security priority also seems to lead to a search for additional partners in foreign policy. In October 2010, President Yanukovich received the President of Venezuela, Hugo Chavez, on an official state visit aiming to explore bilateral cooperation between Ukraine and Venezuela. The main issues of common interest were reported to be the export of Venezuelan oil and gas and possible arms deals. These steps for rapprochement between Venezuela and Ukraine resemble more the stance of Belarus than the position of a country aiming to align itself with the EU.

In addition to general analyses, we need to look at more specific and clear indicators for convergence or divergence with the EU in foreign policy. Barbé *et al.* (2009, p. 839) have used the rate of alignment with EU foreign-policy acts as an indicator for convergence with the EU. The most important EU foreign-policy acts are decisions, which have replaced the CFSP common positions, actions and decisions since the Lisbon Treaty came into force in December 2009.

Alignment with EU declarations can also be taken into account as a symbolic allegiance to EU policies. Barbé *et al.* have rightly noted (2009, p. 839) that alignment with declarations is not very costly for third countries and can be done easily, especially when countries do not have a position on the issue in question. If countries do have a position on an issue, however, we would see failure to align with an EU declaration as significant.

---

[13]Razumkov Centre, 'What is Hidden Behind the Change of Foreign Policy Guidelines?', available at: www.razumkov.org.ua, accessed 4 February 2011.

[14]Razumkov Centre, 'What is Hidden Behind the Change of Foreign Policy Guidelines?', available at: www.razumkov.org.ua, accessed 4 February 2011.

[15]Razumkov Centre, 'What is Hidden Behind the Change of Foreign Policy Guidelines?', available at: www.razumkov.org.ua, accessed 4 February 2011.

[16]As witnessed by the president's yearly report to the *Rada* in 2010 where the issue of energy security is discussed on an equal footing with relations with neighbours and regional integration. See the official report to the parliament (in Ukrainian), available at: http://www.president.gov.ua/documents/, accessed 7 September 2011.

Data from Ukraine's Razumkov Centre show that in 2007 Ukraine had aligned itself with 92% of CFSP statements (Dimitrova & Dragneva 2009, p. 862). The European Commission, in its last progress report on the implementation of Ukraine's ENP Action Plan, also expressed satisfaction that Ukraine had aligned itself with 'most CFSP declarations open for alignment' (European Commission, 2010a, p. 6).

The exceptions—the cases in which Ukraine has not aligned itself with EU sanctions— are telling as they are related to key EU measures, sanctions where Ukraine's stance could actually make a difference. In October 2010, for example, following the suppression of protest and the abuse of arrested protesters in Belarus in the aftermath of the presidential elections, the EU adopted Council Decision 2010/639/CFSP[17] on sanctions for Belarus officials. Ukraine did not align itself with the EU's position in this case. In previous years, Ukraine has also refrained from joining EU sanctions on Belarus officials.

The situation in 2011 is already suggestive of a changing trend whereby Ukraine has aligned with fewer EU measures. Ukraine has not aligned itself with most of the EU's decisions on sanctions so far, as seen from Table 1.

To provide some basis for comparison of these results, we note that Moldova and Armenia, for example, have aligned themselves with EU decisions on restrictive measures on Tunisia, Zimbabwe, Cote D'Ivoire and Iraq, but not on Belarus.

To summarise, in foreign policy we find moderate convergence overall, with some important exceptions and a decreasing trend since 2010. This is evident at the level of rhetorical convergence and symbolism in high politics, based on the declared foreign policy

TABLE 1

ALIGNMENT OF UKRAINE WITH EU DECISIONS ON SANCTIONS WITH THIRD COUNTRIES IN 2011

Year	EU measures	Countries and persons targeted by sanctions	Ukrainian alignment
2011	Council Decision 2010/656/CFSP; Council Decision 2010/801; Council Decision 2011/17/CFSP; Council Decision 2011/18/CFSP; and Council Decision 2011/71/CFSP	Cote d'Ivoire	No
2011	Council Decision 2011/69/CFSP; Council Decision 2010/639/CFSP	Belarus	No
2011	Council Decision 2011/70/CFSP updating the list of persons, groups and entities subject to Articles 2, 3 and 4 of Common Position 2001/931/CFSP on the application of specific measures to combat terrorism	List of persons on subject to measures combating terrorism	Yes
2011	Council Decision 2011/72/CFSP; Council implementing Decision 2011/79/CFSP	Tunisia, misappropriation of state funds	No
2011	Council Decision 2011/101/CFSP	Zimbabwe	No
2011	Council Decision 2011/100/CFSP amending Common Position 2003/495/CFSP on Iraq	Iraq	No

Source: Compiled by the authors based on Council of Ministers data, available at: http://www.consilium.europa.eu/App/newsroom/loadbook.aspx?BID = 73&LANG = 1&cmsid = 257, accessed 8 October 2011.

[17]Council Decision 2010/639/CFSP, *Official Journal of the European Union*, 26 October 2010.

priorities and the actions of the Yanukovich administration in 2010 and 2011, as well as at the level of convergence with specific EU measures towards third countries. In terms of behavioural convergence, Ukraine's participation in EU missions remains the same, even though we must note that the operations and Ukraine's part in them are quite small. Thus, we have a mixed picture that suggests less convergence at the level of rhetoric (and especially in high politics) under Yanukovich, combined with continued behavioural compliance at the operational level.

Our interpretation of this mixed picture of convergence with EU demands within foreign and security policy highlights two important factors, consistent with our framework. The first one is the existence of specific incentives for some informal veto players, such as gas and coal oligarchs, to accommodate Russia's position, and Russia's tendency to create issue linkages between gas and geopolitics. The second is that convergence with most of the EU's measures and actions in CFSP and ESDP is not very costly for the Ukrainian leadership in terms of electoral support or resources. Alignment with EU sanctions against Belarus, with which Ukraine has considerable ties in the context of Russia's symbolic Eastern orthodox community, would be however, even more costly for the president than it was to the previous administration (which also refrained from supporting these sanctions and declarations), and remains an area of divergence with the EU.

The next section will examine this situation in relation to state aid, an internal market-related policy where, arguably, a different actor constellation affects policy convergence.

State aid regulation

Demands for convergence in the area of state aid have been high on the list of the EU's priorities and have required extensive legal and institutional changes. Convergence in this field requires changes in legislation to establish parameters for lawful state aid as well as in institutional structures and administrative practices to ensure monitoring of the state authorities engaged in state aid, and the recovery of unlawfully granted aid.

Starting with the PCA, which entered into force in 1998, state aid has been one of the EU's priority areas for legislative convergence. The PCA required Ukraine not just to refrain from granting state aid that is likely to affect trade between Ukraine and the EU, but also the voluntary adoption by Ukraine of the EU's *acquis* in the area of competition law (including state aid). The EU–Ukraine Action Plan of 2005 similarly identified state aid as a key area for development.[18] This is understandable given the centrality of state aid in the functioning of the internal market and the maintenance of competitive conditions in the EU as well as the definition of a 'stake in the internal market' as one of the key rewards of the ENP. In fact, state aid is one of the few areas where the Action Plan referred to the specific EU *acquis* and required measures such as the adoption of a definition of state aid compatible with that of the EU, the establishment of transparency mechanisms as regards the state aid granted, as well as an independent surveillance body and procedures for regular reporting on the aid granted.[19] Importantly, state aid is one of the thematic areas for negotiation within the

---

[18]For an overview of the ENP instruments, including the Action Plans and other official documents, see: http://ec.europa.eu/world/enp/documents_en.htm#2, accessed 22 June 2012.

[19]Section 39 of the EU–Ukraine Action Plan.

Association Agreement[20] in relation to the DCFTA. Reform of state aid practices related to trade were also subject to reform in the context of Ukraine's preparation for accession to the WTO which took place in May 2008. A key aspect of this preparation was the elimination of subsidies prohibited under the WTO Agreement on Subsidies and Countervailing Measures.

Despite the high priority attached to the area of state aid and competition by the EU and WTO, however, progress in convergence has been slow.[21] While our primary interest relates to the period marked by the arrival of Yanukovich's presidency, we look back and highlight some key steps in convergence since the early 2000s. This is critical given that later developments show important continuities and are arguably less about convergence and more about battles over the *status quo* (particularly in relation to control over the Anti-Monopoly Committee (AMC)).

First legislative convergence in the field remains very partial and highly fragmented (Table 2). The 2001 Law on Competition and the 2003 Economic Code are the key laws that deal with some of the EU requirements, yet they reflect EU norms only in part and lack detail. Furthermore, the norms of the Economic Code in particular have been embedded in a wider framework promoting the principle of state interference in the economy rather than limiting it (Shishkin & Drobishev 2007; OECD 2007). In fact, repealing the Economic Code has become an important pressure point for most external stakeholders and is a specific item in the EU–Ukraine Action Plan of 2005.

There have been two main legislative attempts to improve the legal basis of the regime, but both failed to be adopted by the *Rada*. Indeed, the failure to adopt a proper legislative framework is indicative of a persistent pattern. In April 2004, Yanukovich's government brought in a draft law on state aid. As the justification of the key drafter, the AMC, shows, the concern was to create a level playing field in the provision of state aid as well as to implement the undertaking for voluntary harmonisation in this field under the PCA.[22] Expert opinion showed that the draft was closely based on EU provisions, despite some shortcomings (ICPS 2007; OECD 2008). Another draft seeking the amendment of the 2001 Law on Competition was submitted by Yanukovich's government in March 2007.[23]

Secondly, there has been little progress in providing an adequate institutional framework for the *ex ante* and *ex post* monitoring of the granting of state aid. State aid, in principle, was granted by a range of agencies (central, local, sectoral or regional) according to various laws and secondary resolutions. Studies of the provision of state aid in Ukraine show that the largest part of state aid was sectoral (70% compared to the EU average of 24%) rather than regional, with steel manufacturing being the highest recipient in 2000, followed later by car manufacturing, pharmaceuticals and especially fuel and energy (crucially in 2003–2005)

---

[20]The Association Agreement is to replace the expired Partnership and Cooperation Agreement (PCA). Association Agreement negotiations had been making little progress in 2010, and there was even the suggestion from some analysts that they were being sabotaged by influential oligarchs who had begun to realise the implications of the free trade area for their businesses (Valasek 2010, p. 5). At the end of 2011 the negotiations on the Agreement were finalised, yet its signing and completion remain stalled.

[21]'Evaluation of the State of Adaptation of the Legislation of Ukraine to the European Acquis until 2008', State Department for Legislative Adaptation, 27 January 2010, available at: http://eurodocs.sdla.gov.ua/DocumentView/tabid/28/ctl/Edit/mid/27/ID/10006025/Lang/Default.aspx, accessed 18 March 2011.

[22]See Explanatory Note of the Anti-Monopoly Committee, available at: http://w1.c1.rada.gov.ua/pls/zweb_n/webproc4_1?id = &pf3511 = 17983, accessed 20 May 2011.

[23]Nonetheless, according to experts, the draft was lacking in a number of important ways, for example in relation to various notification requirements or the mechanisms for recovery of unlawfully granted aid (OECD 2008, p. 41).

TABLE 2

ALIGNMENT OF UKRAINIAN LEGISLATION WITH KEY EU ACQUIS ON STATE AID

EU legislation	Alignment
Article 87 TEC	Partial: Article 15 Law on Protection of Economic Competition (2001), Article 26 European Code (2003)
Article 88 TEC	No
Article 89 TEC	No
Council Regulation (EC) No. 994/98 of 7 May 1998 on the application of Articles 92 and 93 of the Treaty establishing the European Community to certain categories of horizontal state aid	Partial: Sectoral secondary legislation
Council Regulation (EC) No. 659/1999 of 22 March 1999 laying down detailed rules for the application of Article 93 of the EC Treaty	No
Commission Regulation (EC) No. 69/2001 of 12 January 2001 on the application of Articles 87 and 88 of the EC Treaty to *de minimis* aid	No
Commission Regulation (EC) No. 70/2001 of 12 January 2001 on the application of Articles 87 and 88 of the EC Treaty to state aid to small and medium-sized enterprises	Partial: Article 48 Economic Code (2003), Article 5 Law on State Support of Small Enterprises (2000), Part II Law on the National Programme to Promote Small Business Development (2000)
Commission Regulation (EC) No. 2204/2002 of 12 December 2002 on the application of Articles 87 and 88 of the EC Treaty to state aid for employment	Partial: Articles 2, 3, 5 Labour Code (1971)
Commission Regulation (EC) No. 68/2001 of 12 January 2001 on the application of Articles 87 and 88 of the EC Treaty to training aid	Partial: Selected provisions in various legal acts
Guidelines on national regional aid for 2007–2013, OJ C 54	Partial: Article 2 Law on Stimulating the Development of Regions (2005) Article 9—contradictory provisions; Article 1 (2) Law on General Principles for the Creation and Functioning of Special (Free) Economic Zones (1992)
Commission Regulation (EC) No. 1628/2006 on the application of Articles 87 and 88 of the EC Treaty to national regional investment aid	No

Source: Authors' compilation based on reports of the Ministry of Justice, available at: www.sdla.gov.ua/control/uk/publish/article?art_id + 47553&cat_id = 46959, accessed 18 March 2011.

(Gazizullin 2006). It was primarily implementing legislation that was the basis for such aid with no clear criteria spelt out for its provision.

Furthermore, while direct subsidies were used, such as to the coal mining industry or the steel industry (between 1999 and 2002) (Legeida 2002; WTO 2008), much of this aid has taken the form of indirect aid, which is opaque and difficult to quantify. Examples from the gas and electricity industry show the extensive and subtle forms of business support ranging from poor collection of cash (debt and tax) arrears to mispricing. While direct subsidies have a clearer connection with the institutional organisation of state aid, indirect subsidies often relate to the quality of governance and the general state of the rule of law in the country.

The WTO accession process gave a boost to some developments in the area of state aid, most notably in relation to the abolition of a range of privileges to the machine-building industry and other industries in 2005 (IERPC 2011). Yet, state support in the form of direct transfers or state guarantees for loans remains high for other sectors, such as coal mining. Tax privileges also persist, as shown in recent budgets.

Even more importantly, the institutional framework for state aid has remained weak. According to the 2001 Competition Law,[24] state agencies were required to seek the view of the AMC on any draft decisions they planned to take that may affect competitive behaviour. Yet, the AMC had very weak powers in asserting prohibition or seeking recovery from an aid recipient if approval was not sought in advance. More importantly, neither piece of legislation sets up a system for recording or monitoring the granting of state aid or entrusts an independent body with the supervision of the process. The AMC could not be deemed to be independent. According to the 1996 Constitution of Ukraine, the Chairman of the AMC was appointed by the president with the consent of the parliament, while the remaining members of the AMC were appointed by the president. While this is not necessarily unique in international practice, certainly in the Ukrainian political context, this dependence matters.

Despite the start of the negotiations on the Association Agreement in 2009, legislative and institutional progress (other than at the level of strategy) is still lacking. An inter-departmental group, which was set up in July 2008 and received EU technical assistance for its work (OECD 2010), produced a Concept on the reform of state aid in January 2010. This act, adopted just before the 2010 presidential elections, sought to provide a framework for convergence of legislation and reform of the system within the next five years. The establishment of a system for monitoring of the state aid granted by central and local authorities was deemed to be a first step in this process, followed by the drafting of a new law on state aid.

During 2010 there was no visible progress in implementing the Concept.[25] In January 2011, Azarov's government adopted some amendments to it. Some of these amendments seem to be consistent with the progress in negotiating the state aid chapter in the Association Agreement, e.g. on the monitoring of state aid through the establishment of inventories of aid schemes (Biegunski 2010). It is clear that a working group has been preparing a new law on state aid for some time, yet, it is difficult to know when and whether this draft will turn into a law.

Given the complexity and sensitivity of state aid regulation, convergence in this field is bound to be difficult. Yet, the story of EU alignment in Ukraine is particularly instructive in showing the critical role of domestic veto players in obstructing it. The most visible aspect here is the opposition of vested interests—our informal veto players—that stand to lose from changes in policy. State support was an important aspect of the state planning paradigms promoted by the Communist Party or the Socialist Party (Wilson 2009), but also of the established oligarchic system of rent-seeking and rent-giving. This system extended state privilege to enterprise managers from non-privatised, 'sensitive' sector companies (e.g. extraction industries), as well as oligarchic groups acquiring such companies through privatisation (e.g. steel and energy distribution), that sought to block unwanted reforms or steer them on privileged terms. As discussed above, many of those oligarchs are represented

---

[24]Article 15(2). For a more extensive discussion, see OECD (2008), pp. 39–41.

[25]Indeed, the EU Progress Report on Implementation of the ENP in 2009, Brussels, 12 May 2010, SEC (2010) 524, notes the breakdown of the intra-departmental group amidst disputes between the ministries on the legal basis for a state aid inventory (available at: http://ec.europa.eu/world/enp/pdf/progress2010/sec10_524_en.pdf, accessed 21 March 2011).

in the Party of Regions, even if oligarchic backing is not unique to that party. Yet, the political representation of oligarchs from the Party of Regions has become even stronger post-2010 because of the Party's current dominance over the *Rada* as well as the presidency.

These oligarchs, have, as informal veto players, opposed legislative changes that could disturb their existing networks of patronage. One such arrangement was the control over and the powers of the AMC. This institution could potentially play a significant role in the alignment with EU norms as related to both drafting new legislation and exercising *ex ante* and *ex post* control over the system of delivery of state aid. Deliberations on the draft law on state aid on 22 December 2004 show that one of the main concerns across oligarchic factions was about the powers of the Committee.[26] Most oligarchic parties, in fact, did not vote in support of the bill. Given that the vote was taking place in the middle of the Orange Revolution, debates show that 'Orange' realignment might have also been a consideration in resisting changes with unknown implications. Indeed, some of the constitutional amendments negotiated in the context of the Orange Revolution, related to limiting the power of the presidency and empowering the *Rada* (based on the government's proposal) in appointing the AMC.

The battle for control over the AMC clearly continues in the recent reversal of the mechanism for appointing the chair of the AMC. The decision of the Constitutional Court of October 2010, the amendments to the Law on the Council of Ministers and the new Law on the Central Organs of Executive Power of 17 March 2011, led to the reversal of the 2004 constitutional settlement and have brought the appointment of the AMC chair back to the presidency. We can see the president and his administration concentrating further power and changing the domestic veto player configuration by changing the institutional rules of the political game. Given that the AMC will be under the control of oligarchic factions connected to the Party of Regions and the president, it is doubtful whether it will have the incentives to limit, or even make transparent, state aid practices.

Further, the importance attributed to controlling the AMC is well illustrated by the battle for its chairmanship. Oleksey Kostuev, who chaired it between 2001 and 2008, was a member of the pro-Kuchma oligarchic Labour Ukraine (*Trudova Ukrayina*) faction in the 1998–2002 *Rada* and switched later to the Party of Regions. As Timoshenko started her second term in government, she sought his replacement in January 2008. This was strongly opposed by the Party of Regions, which blocked several new appointments.[27] It was only in April 2010 (in the aftermath of President Yanukovich's victory and in the advent of Azarov's government) that a head of the AMC was formally appointed and that was again Kostuev.[28]

What is less visible, but no less important, is the broader opposition to the change of a system of rent-seeking as such and the implementation of legal and institutional reform directed to greater transparency and good governance. Given the prominence of indirect subsidies this is certainly the more difficult aspect of EU alignment. For example, recent

[26]See http://static.rada.gov.ua/zakon/skl4/6session/STENOGR/22120406_57.htm, accessed 20 May 2011.

[27]Timoshenko proposed David Zhvania in March 2008 and Volodimir Karetka in October 2009; see archive of the *Rada*, available at: http://portal.rada.gov.ua, accessed 10 September 2011.

[28]Kostuev left in 2010 to become the Mayor of Odessa, and was followed by Vasil Tsushko from the Socialist Party, who was prior to that in charge of the Economic Ministry in Azarov's government. The 'Orange' parties, Block Yulia Timoshenko (*Blok Yuliyi Tymoshenko*) and Our Ukraine (*Nasha Ukrayina*), opposed both nominations.

media reports point to key oligarchs linked to the Party of Regions as the worst public debtors in Ukraine.[29]

A final twist in the story of state aid legislation is provided by confusion as to what such legislation would actually mean and do. References to 'state aid' have sometimes been used as a substitute for 'state interference' and signified opposition to market-based reform. During the first reading of the draft law on state aid of 22 December 2004, for example, the representatives of the Communist Party supported the bill referring to its role in state support of businesses (even if within a framework of enhanced transparency and non-discrimination), and as a continuation of the principles set by the Economic Code.[30] Statements in this debate clearly view state enterprises rather than private business as the legitimate recipients of such aid. In reaction to this, Viktor Pynzenyk, a known reformer representing Our Ukraine's faction in this convocation of the *Rada*, delivered a damning evaluation of the law as legitimising a rent-provision mechanism, stating that the proper name of this law should actually be law 'about the legality of corruption'.[31] To summarise, convergence with EU policy or EU demands on state aid and passing the appropriate legislation has not been a priority for reform in Ukraine for formal and informal veto players, and those who have been in favour of passing the draft law on state aid have actually misunderstood what it was meant to accomplish. Further, others, like Pynzenyk, did not view this law in relation to technocratic alignment with EU norms, but in the broader terms of how it affects the political and economic system of distribution of resources in the country.

Conclusions

In this essay we have presented a domestic, veto-player driven explanation of the limited convergence with the EU in two policy areas. Our explanation builds on existing Europeanisation approaches, especially on literature that emphasises domestic actors' cost–benefit calculations (Schimmelfennig & Sedelmeier 2005) and those who focus on specific sectors (Ademmer & Börzel; Buzogány; Langbein, in this collection). In contrast to the way veto-player explanations have been used in the Europeanisation literature so far, and following Dimitrova (2010), we explicitly focus on the role of informal veto players. Thus our analysis allows us to take into account key features of the Ukrainian political system, such as the interpenetration of economic and political elites. We argue that these elites have had preferences aimed at the preservation of the *status quo* which made convergence difficult when it affected their interests.

Our review of domestic developments in Ukraine in two sectors—foreign policy and state aid—has confirmed that oligarchic groups have indeed been critical in policy making in Ukraine, including convergence (or non-convergence) with EU norms. The two policy areas under investigation illustrate this point very clearly. In state aid, convergence with the EU

---

[29]Certainly Aleksander Savchuk from the Party of Regions and Dmitri Firtash, one of its key backers, feature prominently on the list; see Dubinskii *et al.* (2010).

[30]Interestingly, at the vote in May 2007 the Communist Party opposed the bill amending the Law on Competition, confirming the importance of 'grand narratives' to this party, i.e. 'competition' compared to 'state aid'.

[31]See records of parliamentary debates on 22 December 2004, available at: http://static.rada.gov.ua/zakon/skl4/6session/STENOGR/22120406_57.htm, accessed 21 March 2011.

acquis can be described more in terms of rhetorical commitment rather than comprehensive legal adoption and compliance. In terms of behavioural compliance, we see that specific parts of the administrative system, such as the state aid regulator, are captured by the rent-seeking system. Thus limited progress is a clear result of the continued opposition of partisan and informal veto players (oligarchic factions and their parliamentary allies). We find that their position is driven not so much by attitudes to EU integration in general, but by the potential losses from policy change.

Most of all, we find that their position is critically linked to control over the political system of rent distribution (or protection from rent losses), as illustrated in the battle for the AMC. This strategic interest can coincide with the ideological component in the preferences of other veto players, such as the Communist Party, resulting in the slow progress in this field. In other words, preservation of gains from state capture will take precedence over policy-specific gains. This suggests some limits to the impact that the EU could make on convergence with policy-specific conditionality.

As for foreign and security policy, there has been moderate progress in convergence in the past, mostly between 2004 and 2009. In this area the change of veto players has led to a clearer change in direction, as we can see by the somewhat increased number of cases where Ukraine avoided formal adoption of EU measures in 2011. In fact, there is so little alignment with EU decisions we can almost speak of a trend reversed. The key player that has been in a position to affect developments here is the president. The gas-for-fleet deal, the main geopolitical decision taken by Yanukovich so far in Ukraine's foreign policy, reflects the interests of informal veto players and the president's own electoral promises. Formal convergence with EU measures such as sanctions is absent when it comes to countries where Ukraine's convergence could really mean something—for example Belarus. We believe this is related to the costs that key actors perceive to be attached to aligning with the EU both in terms of trade and in terms of the symbolic relationship with Russia. The importance attached by Russia under Putin on the fraternity links between Russia, Ukraine and Belarus means that it matters to both Russia and Belarus whether Ukraine joins the EU sanctions on Belarus or not. For this reason, we consider support for the EU's sanctions against Belarus to be costly for Yanukovich. By contrast, participation in peacekeeping operations is relatively low cost for the Ukrainian government given that the EU's operations are relatively small and that Ukraine maintains significant armed forces anyway. This difference in domestic costs in convergence, political, electoral and economic fields, explains, according to us, the differential convergence in foreign policy and peacekeeping.

Based on the above comparison within and between policy sectors, we show that in policy areas where convergence with EU rules can affect negatively the interests of oligarchs and their political allies, we see only limited policy change. This is regardless of whether the area in question is part of the core EU *acquis* or not. The example of state aid makes this quite clear. Furthermore, even if substantive provisions of the *acquis* are formally adopted, the 'technocratic' external governance reforms can be effective only if the very core of the system dominated by rent-seeking and competitive oligarchy is also changed. There is no evidence that this is currently the case. The developments in 2010 and the spring of 2011 show further concentration of power in Ukraine's political system behind the president, the Party of Regions and the oligarchic factions mentioned above.

Ultimately, our findings confirm the importance of domestic actors' preferences and the weakened role of the kind of external incentives—economic and symbolic—that the EU offers at this point. If the EU wants to be successful in promoting reforms in Ukraine in a particular direction, it needs to look at and deal with the relevant domestic actor constellations. In this sense, our conclusions reinforce the argument that the EU should offer specific and stronger incentives such as visa liberalisation and develop policy conditionality linked to progress in specific areas (Ademmer & Börzel; Buzogány, in this collection). Policy conditionality is defined, following Ademmer and Börzel (in this collection), as policy-specific positive and negative incentives. Provided that the rules the EU aims to promote do not affect state capture, targeted policy conditionality may be successful.

Alternatively, a more robust EU approach might aim to diminish the levels of state capture by stressing good governance reforms—a path which becomes increasingly problematic given the shape of Ukraine's political system at present. Even though it requires a level of commitment which the EU of today cannot achieve, this is ultimately the only path that will prevent informal veto players from using the Ukrainian state and political system for their own gain and from vetoing any policy change that may limit their autonomy.

Leiden University
The University of Birmingham

References

Barbé, E., Costa, O., Surrallés, A. H. & Natorski, M. (2009) 'Which Rules Shape EU External Governance? Patterns of Rule Selection in Foreign and Security Policies', *Journal of European Public Policy*, 16, p. 6.

Biegunski, L. (2010) 'Concept of Ukrainian Law on State Aid Control', available at: http://competitionproject.org.ua/images/stories/document/Concept_of_State_Aid_.pdf, accessed 19 March 2011.

Ćwiek-Karpowicz, J. (2010) 'Russia–Ukraine Agreements on Black Sea Fleet Stationing and Preferential Gas Prices', Bulletin No. 62 (138), 23 April (Polish Institute of International Affairs (PISM)), available at: http://www.pism.pl/index/?id=7a5200e5e9b3a893e1c2b0ccba7dd72f, accessed 15 November 2012.

D'Anieri, P. (2007) *Understanding Ukrainian Politics: Power, Politics and Institutional Design* (Armonk, NY, ME Sharpe).

Darden, K. (2001) 'Blackmail as a Tool of State Domination: Ukraine under Kuchma', *East European Constitutional Review*, 10, 67.

Dimitrova, A. (2004) 'Introduction: Driven to Change: The European Union's Enlargement Viewed from the East', in Dimitrova, A. (ed.) (2004) *Driven to Change: The European Union's Enlargement Viewed from the East* (Manchester, Manchester University Press).

Dimitrova, A. (2010) 'The New Member States of the EU in the Aftermath of Enlargement: Do New European Rules Remain Empty Shells?', *Journal of European Public Policy*, 17, 1.

Dimitrova, A. & Dragneva, R. (2009) 'Constraining External Governance: Interdependence with Russia and the CIS as Limits to the EU's Rule Transfer in the Ukraine', *Journal of European Public Policy*, 16, 6.

Dragneva, R. & Dimitrova, A. (2010) 'The Politics of Demand for Law: The Case of Ukraine's Company Law Reform', *European Journal of Law Reform*, 12, 3–4.

Dubinskii, A., Pasochnik, V. & Skolotianiy, I. (2010) 'Reiting Skandal'nykh dolzhnikov', *Zerkalo Nedely*, 25 September, available at: http://zn.ua/ECONOMICS/reyting_skandalnyh_dolzhnikov-61107.html, accessed 29 September 2011.

European Commission (2004) *Commission Staff Working Paper, European Neighbourhood Policy, Country Report Ukraine*, COM (2004) 373 Final (Brussels), available at: http://ec.europa.eu/world/enp/pdf/strategy/strategy_paper_en.pdf, accessed 25 June 2012.

European Commission (2006) *Communication from the Commission to the Council and the European Parliament on Strengthening of the European Neighbourhood Policy*, COM (2006) 726 Final (Brussels), available at: http://ec.europa.eu/world/enp/pdf/com06_726_en.pdf, accessed 25 June 2012.

European Commission (2010a) *Commission Staff Working Document Accompanying the Communication from the Commission to the European Parliament and the Council: Taking Stock of the European Neighbourhood Policy (ENP), Implementation of the European Neighbourhood Policy in 2009; Progress Report Ukraine*, 12 May, SEC (2010) 524 (Brussels), available at: http://ec.europa.eu/world/enp/pdf/progress2010/sec10_524_en.pdf, accessed 25 June 2012.

European Commission (2010b) *Commission Staff Working Document Accompanying the Communication from the Commission to the European Parliament and the Council: Taking Stock of the European Neighbourhood Policy (ENP), Implementation of the European Neighbourhood Policy in 2009, Progress Report Ukraine*, COM (2010) 207 Final (Brussels), available at: http://eur-lex.europa.eu/LexUriServ/LexUriServ.do?uri=COM:2010:0207:FIN:EN:PDF, accessed 25 June 2012.

Fink Hafner, D. (1999) 'Dilemmas in Managing the Expanding EU: The EU and Applicant States' Points of View', *Journal of European Public Policy*, 6, 5.

Flikke, G. (2008) 'Pacts, Parties and Elite Struggle: Ukraine's Troubled Post-Orange Transition', *Europe-Asia Studies*, 60, 3.

'Fourth Joint Progress Report on the Negotiations on the EU–Ukraine Association Agreement', Brussels, Kyiv, 8 November 2010.

Freyburg, T., Lavenex, S., Schimmelfennig, F., Skripka, T. & Wetzel, A. (2009) 'EU Promotion of Democratic Governance in the Neighbourhood', *Journal of European Public Policy*, 16, 6.

Ganev, V. (2007) *Preying on the State: The Transformation of Bulgaria after 1989* (Ithaca, NY & London, Cornell University Press).

Gazizullin, I. (2006) *State Aid in Ukraine: Practice and Challenges*, INDEUNIS Papers, September, available at: http://www.icps.com.ua/files/articles/46/71/State%20aid_ICPS_edited.pdf, accessed 10 February 2011.

Hale, J. (2010) 'EU Notes: Offsets, Military Projects, Ukrainian Troops', *Defense News*, 11 November, available at: www.defensenews.com/story.php?i=3809001, accessed 12 February 2011.

Handrich, L., Ferdinand, P. & Poltavets, I. (2003) *Ukrainian Steam Coal: Not Competitive or Just Mismanaged?* Institute for Economic Research and Policy Consulting, December, available at: http://www.ier.com.ua/files/publications/Policy_papers/German_advisory_group/2003/T19_eng.pdf, accessed 7 February 2011.

Hellman, J. (1998) 'Winners Take All: The Politics of Partial Reform in Post-communist Transitions', *World Politics*, 50, 203.

Henderson, K. (ed.) (1999) *Back to Europe: Central and Eastern Europe and the European Union* (London & Philadelphia, PA, UCL Press).

Institute for Economic Research and Policy Consulting (IERPC) (2011) *Costs and Benefits of FTA Between Ukraine and the European Union*, available at: http://www.ier.com.ua/en/publications/books/?pid=2633, accessed 10 February 2011.

International Centre for Policy Studies (ICPS) (2007) *Free Trade Between Ukraine and the EU; An Impact Assessment*, available at: http://www.pasos.org/content/download/10499/69123/file/FTA_Impact_E.pdf, accessed 10 February 2011.

Kelley, J. (2006) 'New Wine in Old Wineskins: Promoting Political Reforms through the New European Neighbourhood Policy', *Journal of Common Market Studies*, 44, 1.

Lange, N. (2010) 'The First 100 Days after Change of Power in Ukraine: Authoritarian Tendencies and Rapprochement with Russia', Country Report, Konrad Adenauer Stiftung, available at: www.kas.de/ukraine, accessed 22 March 2011.

Lavenex, S. (2008) 'A Governance Perspective on the European Neighbourhood Policy: Integration beyond Conditionality?', *Journal of European Public Policy*, 15, 6.

Lavenex, S. & Schimmelfennig, F. (2009) 'EU Rules beyond EU Borders: Theorizing External Governance in European Politics', *Journal of European Public Policy*, 16, 6.

Legeida, N. (2002) *The Economic Implications of Government Support for the Steel Industry: The Case of Ukraine*, (Institute for Economic Research and Policy Consulting, Working Paper No. 16), available at: http://pdc.ceu.hu/archive/00001668/01/WP_16_eng.pdf, accessed 10 February 2011.

Malygina, K. (2010) 'Ukraine as a Neo-Patrimonial State: Understanding Political Change in Ukraine in 2005–2010', *SEER Journal of Labour and Social Affairs in Eastern Europe*, 1, available at: http://www.seer.nomos.de/fileadmin/seer/doc/Aufsatz_SEER_10_01.pdf, accessed 5 February 2011.

Marone, J. (2010) 'Gas Man Firtash on the Rise Again in Yanukovich Era', *Kyivpost*, 9 April, available at: http://www.kyivpost.com/news/nation/detail/63494/, accessed 3 September 2011.

Martsynovski, A. (2011) 'After Belarus Sanctions, What About Ukraine?', *EU Observer*, available at: www.euobserver.com, accessed 6 February 2011.

Matuszak, S. (2011) 'How Ukrainian Oligarchs View Economic Integration with the EU and Russia', *EastWeek, Centre for Eastern Studies*, available at: http://www.osw.waw.pl/en/publikacje/eastweek/2011-09-14/how-ukrainian-oligarchs-view-economic-integration-eu-and-russia, accessed 26 September 2011.

Melnykovska, I. & Schweickert, R. (2008) 'Bottom Up or Top Down: What Drives the Convergence of Ukraine's Institutions Towards European Standards?', *Southeast European and Black Sea Studies*, 8, 4.

Moravcsik, A. (1998) *The Choice for Europe: Social Purpose and State Power from Messina to Maastricht* (Ithaca, NY, Cornell University Press).

OECD (2007) 'Economic Surveys, Ukraine: Economic Assessment', available at: http://www.oecd.org/dataoecd/26/0/39196918.pdf, accessed 4 September 2011.

OECD (2008) 'Competition Law and Policy in Ukraine: An OECD Peer Review', available at: http://www.oecd.org/dataoecd/44/26/41165857.pdf, accessed 2 September 2011.

OECD (2010) 'Competition, State Aids and Subsidies: Contribution from Ukraine', 11 January, available at: http://www.oecd.org/dataoecd/52/47/44377890.pdf, accessed 19 March 2011.

Polese, A. (2009) 'Ukraine 2004: Informal Networks, Transformation of Social Capital and Coloured Revolutions', *Journal of Communist Studies and Transition Politics*, 25, 2.

Pop, V. (2011) 'EU Moots Greater Role in Deals with Oil-rich Countries', *EU Observer*, 8 September, available at: http://euobserver.com/19/113551, accessed 8 September 2011.

Popescu, N. & Wilson, A. (2009) 'The Limits of Enlargement-Lite: European and Russian Power in the Troubled Neighbourhood', Policy Report, European Council of Foreign Relations (London, ECFR).

Puglisi, R. (2003) 'The Rise of Ukrainian Oligarchs', *Democratization*, 10, 3.

Puglisi, R. (2008) 'A Window to the World? Oligarchs and Foreign Policy in Ukraine', in Fischer, S. (ed.) (2008) *Ukraine Quo Vadis?* Chaillot Paper No. 108 (Paris, Institute for Security Studies, EU).

Rehn, O. (2006) 'European Commissioner for Enlargement 'Enlargement Package 2006', presentation in front of the European Parliament's Foreign Affairs Committee', 21 November, Speech 06/727, available at: http://europa.eu/rapid/pressReleasesAction.do?reference=SPEECH/06/727&format=HTML&aged=0&language=EN&guiLanguage=en, accessed 15 November 2012.

Rehn, O. (2007) 'European Commissioner for Enlargement 'What's the Future for EU Enlargement?' speech delivered at the German Marshall Fund of the United States', 25 September, Speech 07/185, available at: http://www.eu-un.europa.eu/articles/es/article_7355_es.htm, accessed 15 November 2012.

Rettman, A. (2011) 'Lukewarm Declaration to Mark the EU Summit in Warsaw', *EU Observer*, available at: http://euobserver.com/24/113696, accessed 22 September 2011.

Schimmelfennig, F. (2001) 'The Community Trap: Liberal Norms, Rhetorical Action and the Eastern Enlargement of the European Union', *International Organization*, 55, 1.

Schimmelfennig, F. & Sedelmeier, U. (eds.) (2005) *The Europeanization of Central and Eastern Europe* (Ithaca and London, Cornell University Press).

Shishkin, S. & Drobyshev, P. (2007) 'Ukraine's Civil and Economic Codes', *Problems of Economic Transition*, 50, 41.

Smolar, E., Presentation at the workshop 'The European Neighbourhood Policy: A Framework for Modernization?', Workshop organised by M. Cremona & W. Sadurski, European University Institute, 1–2 December (Badia Fiesolana, EUI).

Stegnyi, O. (2011) 'Ukraine and the Eastern Partnership: "Lost in Translation?"', *Journal of Communist Studies and Transition Politics*, 27, 1.

Steunenberg, B. & Dimitrova, A. (2007) 'Compliance in the EU Enlargement Process: The Limits of Conditionality', *European Integration online Papers* (EIoP), 11, 5, available at: http://eiop.or.at/eiop/texte/2007-005a.htm, accessed 6 October 2011.

Tsebelis, G. (2002) *Veto Players: How Political Institutions Work* (Princeton, NJ, Princeton University Press).

Vachudova, M. (2005) *Europe Undivided: Democracy, Leverage and Integration after Communism* (Oxford, Oxford University Press).

Valasek, T. (2010) 'Ukraine Turns Away from Democracy and the EU', *CER Policy Brief*, October, available at: www.cer.org.uk, accessed 22 March 2011.

Veselovsky, A. (2008) 'European Integration is for the Worthy', *Zerkalo Nedeli*, 43, (722), 15–21 November, available at: http://www.mw.ua/1000/1550/64718/, accessed 2 February 2011.

Way, L. (2004) 'The Sources and Dynamics of Competitive Authoritarianism in Ukraine', *Journal of Communist Studies and Transition Politics*, 20, 143.

White, S. & McAllister, I. (2009) 'Rethinking the Orange Revolution', *Journal of Communist Studies and Transition Politics*, 25, 2.

Wilson, A. (2009) *Ukrainian: An Unexpected Nation* (New Haven, CT & London, Yale University Press).

Wilson, A. (2010) 'What are the Ukrainians Playing at?', Commentary, European Council of Foreign Relations, 30 April, available at: www.ecfr.eu, accessed 6 September 2011.

Wilson, A. (2011) 'Happy Birthday, Ukraine?', Commentary, European Council of Foreign Relations, 11 August, available at: www.ecfr.eu, accessed 6 September 2011.

Wolczuk, K. (2004) *Integration without Europeanization: Ukraine and its Policy Towards the European Union*, RSCAS Working Paper No. 2004/15, European University Institute, Robert Schuman Centre for Advanced Studies, Badia Fiesolana, San Domenico di Fiesole, Italy.

WTO (2008) *Report of the Working Party on the Accession of Ukraine to the WTO*, WT/AAC/UKR/152, 25 January, available at: http://docsonline.wto.org/DDFDocuments/t/wt/acc/ukr152.doc, accessed 25 September 2011.

Index

Note:
Figures and illustrations are in italics.
Tables in bold.

For Product Safety Concerns and Information please contact our EU representative GPSR@taylorandfrancis.com Taylor & Francis Verlag GmbH, Kaufingerstraße 24, 80331 München, Germany

Batch number: 08165860

Printed by Printforce, the Netherlands